God Bless
Bill Virdon

Copyright 2002 by William Wilson. All rights reserved.

Scripture quotations, unless otherwise noted, are taken from the Holy Bible, New International Version (NIV), copyright 1973, 1978, 1979 by International Bible Society; Scripture quotations marked NKJV are taken from the New King James Version copyright by Thomas Nelson Publishers. Scripture quotations marked NLT are taken from the New Living Translation, copyright 1996 by Tyndale House Publishers.

Printed in the United States of America

ISBN 0-9712311-3-3

VMI Publishers
Sisters, Oregon

This project is dedicated to...
My remarkable wife, Joy, who has inspired and assisted me in keeping life in order; my wonderful children, Phil, Jenelle, Christy, Jeff and Kimberly who have been my cheerleaders in ministry and kept me real; my godly parents, Ruben and Laura Wilson, who instilled in me the ways of the Lord; my wife's parents, Handel and Florence Price, who encouraged me to believe God for miracles; my outstanding pastoral team who has assisted me in fulfilling God's call for my life and the church; my accountability partner's, Rick McPherson and Jim Swanson, who have encouraged me in my daily walk; and to the loving people of Portland Christian Center, who have allowed me the privilege to be their Pastor and friend.

A special thanks...
To Namoi Inman, who worked countless hours with me on the manuscript;
To Katie Gilman, who has served as my executive assistant during this project;
To Greg and Shawn Strannigan, for their insightful editing of this book;
To Bill and Nancie Carmichael and the team at VMI Publishers for their patience, encouragement, and coaching.

CONTENTS

Introduction		7
Chapter One	Knowing God Loves You	11
Chapter Two	Expressing Your Love to God	25
Chapter Three	Learning to Enjoy God's Blessing	43
Chapter Four	Marriage: Pulling Together When You Are Pulling Apart	59
Chapter Five	The Refining Fire of God	79
Chapter Six	It Pays to Tithe	91
Chapter Seven	The Rewards of Serving Jesus	107
Chapter Eight	Living Today In Light of Tomorrow	125

INTRODUCTION

The year . . . 1929. The place . . . Pasadena, California. The event . . . the Rose Bowl, which featured a match up between the number one and two ranked college football teams in the country. The entire nation eagerly awaited the outcome of the battle between Georgia Tech and the University of California.

True to form, these evenly matched rivals played to a standstill throughout most of the first half. With the score tied at 6-6, the nation held its breath, wondering which team would emerge victorious.

And then it happened; the infamous play that determined the outcome of the entire game.

Georgia Tech had possession at their own 30-yard line when their quarterback fumbled the football. Fans cheered wildly as pandemonium erupted on the field. Players from each team scrambled to recover the ball. In the midst of the chaos, one player emerged from the pack. Roy Regals cradled the football in his arms and started the sprint of his life. The clear path to the goal line sent his adrenaline surging.

Roy crossed the 35, then the 40-yard line. He flew past the 50, cleared the 40, and noted with pride that he'd outrun all the Georgia Tech players. Glory awaited him as he rushed toward the end zone. Roy knew the victory was his.

Urged onward by the roar of the crowd, Roy could almost envision tomorrow's headlines: "Regals wins Rose Bowl for Cal." His daydreams were rudely interrupted, however, when he was tackled from behind at the one-yard line. The culprit? His own team mate. The reason? Roy had been running the wrong way.

In all the excitement of the fumble recovery, he'd gotten turned around and headed for his own goal. Roy's misguided run placed his team in jeopardy and ultimately cost them the game. Georgia Tech walked away with an 8-6 victory. Instead of being the hero of tomorrow's headlines, Regals went down in sports history as "Wrong-way Roy."

What instructions do you suppose Roy's coach was shouting at him during that fateful run?

"Turn around, you're going the wrong way!" would be a safe bet.

Which brings us to the prophet Malachi.

PORTRAIT OF A PROPHET

Malachi was the last of a long procession of Old Testament prophets. Like Roy Regal's coach, his primary message to the children of Israel was, "Turn around!"—which literally means "repent". Malachi's name means "my messenger," and God sent this bold prophet to tell His people that they had picked up the ball and were running the wrong way. The children of Israel may have been going through the proper motions, but were headed in the wrong direction.

And they didn't have a clue.

But Malachi did. As a prophet, he had the unique advantage of seeing their situation from God's perspective. He saw past their religious veneer to the true condition of their hearts. Malachi exposed the insolence and indifference that so greatly grieved the heart of God.

Like the prophets before him, Malachi spoke God's words with intensity. Prophets are passionate about the truth. They bring correction to those who wander and comfort to all who turn back to God. Malachi's words are as applicable to our generation as they were to his.

Most scholars believe the book of Malachi was written around 450 BC. By this time, the Israelites had returned from the Babylonian exile and were settled in the land of Palestine. Even with the religious and political reforms instituted by Nehemiah and Ezra, Israel had slipped back into serious spiritual decline. Idolatry and immorality abounded in Malachi's day.

The hard-hearted children of Israel chose not to learn from the mistakes of the past. They questioned not only God's dealings with them, but even His everlasting love. In the book of Malachi, the prophet addresses several questions asked by the Israelites. Through His messenger, God exposes their hearts and calls them to repent and turn back to Him.

But, oddly enough, God begins His message of rebuke with a declaration of His love.

CHAPTER ONE

KNOWING GOD LOVES YOU

MALACHI 1:1-5

"I have loved you," says the Lord.
"Yet you say, 'In what way have You loved us?'"
Mal. 1:1-2 NLT

As a pastor, I must constantly bring people back to the foundation of God's love. Several years ago, I met with a young woman who struggled with an eating disorder. Her problem was rooted in the lie that she was not lovable—she certainly didn't like herself. We opened the Bible, and I spent that rainy afternoon pointing out verses that affirmed God's unconditional love for her. Through the Word, I assured her that God's love did not fluctuate like the numbers on her scale. Even though this girl had grown up in the church, her faith had not been built on the foundation of His unfailing love. It was my privilege as her pastor to establish that truth in her life.

Such was Malachi's calling. Imagine with me the Jerusalem of his day. More than a hundred years earlier, God had judged His people, using the Babylonian empire as the instrument of His will. Babylon conquered the nation of Israel, leveling the great city of Jerusalem. The once proud and prosperous Israelites were bound and taken into captivity.

Mercifully, God's discipline doesn't last forever. After seventy years of slavery in Babylon, God restored His chosen people to their homeland. But the returning Hebrews found Jerusalem in shambles. The ruins which now surrounded them served as a painful reminder of the glory from which they had fallen. Under Nehemiah, the walls of the city were rebuilt. But when the temple was completed, the people wept because it didn't compare with the glory of the original temple that had been destroyed.

That's where God begins with His message through Malachi. He starts to rebuild relationship with His people by laying the foundation of His unfailing love.

Malachi was not the first prophet—nor will he be the last—to speak God's heart of love to His children. In Deuteronomy 10:15, the Lord encourages Moses as he leads the rebellious Israelites through the wilderness. The Updated New

American Standard Version puts this way, "Yet on your fathers did the Lord set His *affection* to love them..." (Note that God not only loves His children, He *likes* them). References to God's love abound throughout the New Testament. 1 John 4:16 clearly defines the nature of God with the simple statement: "God is love." The New Testament culminates with the Wedding Supper of the Lamb, the ultimate celebration of the love of God.

THE QUESTION

"Yet you say, 'In what way have You loved us?'"
Malachi 1:2

"You don't love me anymore!"

What child hasn't uttered—or thought—these words when they haven't gotten their way?

I remember such an incident during our son's middle school years. After disciplining Phil for a particular offense, he came back with the classic response: "You don't love me anymore, so I'm running away!" Wise parents that we were, we helped our young delinquent pack his bags and showed him to the door.

"Don't forget that we love you!" we offered reassuringly as he slung his hastily stuffed backpack over his shoulder.

Thankfully, somewhere between the front door and the end of our street, a great deal of maturity took place in Phil's heart. Within minutes, the door slowly opened. Phil let his backpack slump to the floor and looked up at me.

"I want to come home, Dad. I know you love me and I'm sorry."

Hebrews 12:5-6 (quoting from Proverbs 3:11-12) says, "My son, do not despise the chastening of the Lord, nor be discouraged when you are rebuked by Him; for whom the Lord loves He chastens." Even when it is done in love, discipline is hard to accept—no matter what our age might be.

The Israelites of Malachi's day didn't appreciate God's discipline any more than my son liked my correction. Their question to God—"In what way have You loved us?"—was only a variation of a theme that has long rumbled around the human heart. It was more of an accusation, really, implying that if God truly loved them, their lives would be filled with the blessings they thought they deserved.

Do you catch the flippant note in their query?

"Yeah, sure, You've loved us. Just look at our city, our surroundings, our lives . . . we've known nothing but hardship. If this is what it means to be the Chosen People, then choose somebody else!"

Are we not the same today? Bankruptcy, cancer, divorce ... when ill winds blow into our lives we begin to question God's goodness; we no longer perceive His love. "Where are You, God?" we cry. "What have we done to deserve this? Don't You love us anymore?"

When I first entered into ministry, I was terrified of the possibility that someone might ask a question about the Bible that I couldn't answer. I dreaded coming to the end of a Sunday school lesson—what if one of the college students asked me a theological question and I had no clue what they were talking about? I actually used to practice what I'd say if someone asked me a question that I couldn't answer. My response went something like this:

"You know, that is a great question! And it deserves a good answer. So, give me some time and I will find an answer that will fully satisfy you."

What I was really thinking was, "I have no idea how to answer that! Give me more time and I'll dig up the answer, or find somebody else who knows!"

God is not threatened by our questions. He is waiting to draw them out, to show us our fears and weaknesses so He can speak to them. Like the Israelites, we may ask the questions with anger or disrespect, but God will always answer according to His nature. He responds with sincerity and love. As Paul writes in 2 Timothy 2:13, "If we are faithless, He remains faithful, for He cannot deny Himself."

THE RESPONSE
GOD'S LOVE IS SOVEREIGN
> *"Was not Esau Jacob's brother?" says the Lord. "Yet Jacob I have loved; but Esau I have hated." (Malachi 1:2-3)*

Malachi begins with one of the more difficult passages in the Bible. This text speaks of the sovereignty of God's love. The word "sovereign" means ultimate or maximum authority. God has supreme authority to love. It is part of His character. It is part of who He is.

That's not the part that we have difficulty with. "Jacob I have loved" – so far, so good. The prophet continues, "but Esau I have hated." Does that concept trouble you? Why would God say that he loves one but hates another?

First of all, this verse does not mean that one boy is going to heaven and one boy is going to hell. This theology is called "unconditional election," or double predestination. In this view, there is no such thing as choice. Flip a coin, if you will—if it's heads, you go to heaven. But if it comes up tails, too bad - you are assigned to hell. God chooses our eternal destination, and we are just along for the ride.

This position undermines evangelism and missions. If God chooses who will be saved and who won't be saved, then why bother to preach the gospel? The Bible teaches that God chooses us, and we choose Him. "God ... desires *all* men to be saved and to come to a knowledge of the truth." (1 Timothy 2:3-4). All means ALL—God longs for *everyone* to be saved. The cashier at the store... the bus driver...the schoolteacher...the postal worker...politicians...the garbage collector – they all have this in common: they matter to God. He loves each of them, and He's not willing that any of them should perish. Christ died for all.

So, how do we interpret this verse? Why does God love Jacob and hate Esau?

The book of Genesis tells their story. Jacob and Esau were twins. The Bible tells us that even before they were born, they were fighting in their mother's womb. As Rebekah wondered at the unusual activity of her unborn sons, God told her that the older would serve the younger. This was contrary to the custom of the day, but God told Jacob and Esau's mother what was going to happen.

Fast-forward 1500 years after their birth. "Jacob" and "Esau" now mean more than the names of two Hebrew boys. They represent two nations, two kingdoms. Jacob becomes identified with Israel, God's chosen people. Esau depicts Edom, a rebellious nation. In His dealings with these two families, the sovereign love of God is on display. He calls, but some refuse to come. God, already knowing who would respond, chose Jacob. He called both Jacob and Esau to love Him, but Esau refused.

It is in the context of God's sovereign love that the word "hate" is used. This word does not denote some childish animosity or emotional hostility. The foundational concept is justice. Ignore the emotional connotations of the term "hate" and think of justice.

God loved Jacob. One writer says, "I don't have difficulty with God hating Esau. What bothers me is this – how could God love Jacob?" Jacob was not especially lovable. He was a schemer and a manipulator. But God saw his potential, and He knew what He could make out of Jacob—the father of a great nation.

And so it is with us. God doesn't see us as we are now—He sees who we are destined to be. God loves us too much to let us remain as we are. Consider for a moment a typical young boy. He's ornery, impatient, and is always in trouble. This boy was mean to his siblings, and he got into fistfights in the alley after school. He talked too much in class, and always wound up on his teacher's bad side.

I knew this young man—his name was Billy Wilson. Mercifully, God saw him not for who he was, but for who he would become. God was listening when that boy got on his knees and prayed, "Dear God, would you forgive me and come into my life?" God heard the cry of his heart, and God changed him, and used him. That's God's sovereign love. He doesn't have to love us – but He does.

So, what do we make of this? When God says, "I have loved you," He is referring to His character. Love defines who He is. The Israelites doubted God's love because of their circumstances. But God's love is not circumstantial. His love endures forever!

If you find yourself in a difficult situation and you begin to question God's love –stop looking at the circumstances. Gaze instead at the character and the heart of God. Your circumstances aren't the proof of God's love.

GOD'S LOVE IS STRONG
> "But Esau I have hated, and laid waste his mountains and his heritage for the jackals of the desert."
> (Malachi 1:3)

God's love is strong. It's not sentimental; it's not sappy or syrupy. His love is an expression of His strength. God's love is so overwhelming, so overcoming, that it uses even obstacles to His will to accomplish His purposes.

God hates evil – it is definitional to who He is. The word "God" and the word "good" come from the same root. God, by definition, is good. Therefore, evil cannot co-exist in His presence. Because God is good, He judges evil. When God judges evil, it is a powerful demonstration of His love.

Let's go back to the concept of hate. We tend to think of it as a negative emotion. But in this context, "hate" can be more accurately interpreted as "to be in opposition to." For example, a good doctor tries to bring health and healing and life to his patients. He will hate any disease that has the potential to destroy human life. A judge loves justice, and therefore hates crime.

Parents hate anything that might pose a threat to their children. When our children were very young, Joy and I made every effort to create a safe environment for them. We installed safety locks on the cabinets and pasted Mr. Yuck stickers on bottles containing toxic ingredients. We buckled our children into car seats when we traveled, and took many other precautions to keep them safe. Why? Because we loved our kids, we tried to keep them from harm.

In verse 3, Malachi is saying that God loves His people so much that He will judge the evil that hurts them. The apostle Paul writes in Romans 12:9, "Abhor (hate) what is evil. Cling to what is good." There it is – the same contrast. "I love Jacob, but I hate Esau." Esau represents whatever resists God and stands in opposition to Him. Jacob represents one who has a heart for God and allows God to change him.

God loves that which is good, and hates (or opposes) that which is evil. His judgment on evil is testimony to the strength of His love. For those who choose the way of Esau and resist, God will turn that person's mountains into a wasteland and his inheritance will be left to the jackals. God's love is sovereign and God's love is strong.

GOD'S LOVE IS STEADFAST

Even though Edom has said, "We have been impoverished, but we will return and build the desolate places." Thus says the Lord of hosts, "They may build, but I will throw down; they shall be called The Territory of Wickedness, and a people against whom the Lord will have indignation forever." (Malachi 1:4)

God's love is steadfast. The key to this passage is the word "always." When Edom (the descendants of Esau, who oppose and resist God) tries to rebuild, God is not pleased. He is adamant about destroying their rebuilding campaign.

The same spiritual dynamic operates in our lives today. Satan's works have been effectively destroyed by the power of the cross. When you give your life to Christ, you overcome the works of the evil one. But Satan doesn't sit back and take defeat lightly. He will try to make a comeback and rebuild his influence in your life. Old behaviors and attitudes pop up. A constant battle rages between the old and the new life.

But the good news is that God's love is steadfast. He is always at work, rooting out and destroying the works of the enemy. No matter how many times Satan tries to rebuild his kingdom in your life, God's love will overcome. And where God's love is present, Satan's domain is doomed.

Don't be surprised when Satan whispers in your ear the same lies he has used for thousands of years. "Though I have been crushed, I will rebuild the ruins." We've all heard his lies: "You're worthless. You've failed. You might as well give in to the old life. Quit this Christian stuff. Trying to follow Christ, trying to tithe, attending church, praying, reading the Bible - forget it. You've failed so many times, who are you kidding? You're just one big failure."

But listen to His still, small voice. "That's a lie from Satan," says the Lord. "I am a steadfast God and I will defeat his reign in your life."

GOD'S LOVE IS SEEKING

> *Your eyes shall see and you shall say, "The Lord is magnified beyond the border of Israel!" (Malachi 1:5)*

> *"For from the rising of the sun, even to its going down, My name shall be great among the Gentiles. In every place incense shall be offered to My name, and a pure offering; for My name shall be great among the nations," says the Lord of hosts. (Malachi 1:11)*

God's love is seeking. People of every tribe and tongue and nation—the Lord God loves them all, and desires them to come to Him. "For God so loved the *world*..." That includes not only you and me, but every human heart!

Through Malachi, God proclaimed that He is a God for *all* the nations, not just Israel. His greatness is universal, and no national border can contain it. The Israelites had two misconceptions about being the Chosen People of God. First, they believed that they were chosen because of some inherent quality in them. However, being God's Chosen People wasn't about them, it was about God. God chose them because of His character, not theirs.

Secondly, they missed the point of being God's chosen people by thinking it was all about them. God blessed them so that they might be a blessing to others. The Jews, rather than being a light of God's love to a lost and hurting world, wanted to keep the blessing to themselves. But God never intended for His love to be confined to national borders, or social boundaries. He desires that all men be saved and come to a knowledge of the truth.

When my daughter Kimberly was a preschooler, she came home from Sunday school one morning and announced, "My lesson today, Daddy, was about God's love for me."

I was intrigued by the sudden pronouncement, and by the effect the lesson had on her. I asked, "Oh, is that right? How much does God love you?"

She took both hands and stretched them straight out, as far as she could reach. Then she said, "God loves me this much, Daddy!"

Have you noticed that children don't have a problem believing in God, or believing that God loves them? Adults, on the other hand, often struggle with these very issues. But this truth concerning the love of God is absolutely foundational to our spiritual health. If we don't really believe that God loves us, we won't trust Him. Friendship with God will elude us. We will perceive His discipline as punishment, and we will wind up deeply disappointed.

As an 18 year-old Bible College student, I struggled to feel close to God. Some days, I just couldn't sense His love for me. During this time, I was traveling with the college choir. We performed a concert at a very small church in Elko, Nevada in May of 1970. There were more people in the choir than there were in the congregation on that Sunday night.

I will never forget that evening. After the concert, we met in the church basement for a time of fellowship. The Holy Spirit's presence permeated the room. The choir members erupted into spontaneous prayer, while I sat alone in the corner of the small fellowship hall. I felt completely detached from the activity around me. Under my breath I prayed, "Lord, I don't sense Your presence in my life at all. If You really love me, would You send just one person over to pray for Me?"

As soon as that simple prayer was uttered, five men walked over to me. They laid their hands on me, and began to pray. It was as if God had sent one person and a back-up force of four others to say, "I really love you Bill, and I will exceed your expectations." That was a pivotal moment for me. There was no doubt that I loved the Lord—I was attending Bible College to prepare for ministry - but my heart had become indifferent to the things of God. I was self-centered, making choices with only Bill Wilson in mind.

That day, God began to refocus my life. I encountered afresh the truth that God really loved me. I will never question God's love again—He sent five guys to pray for me when I only asked for one! That spontaneous, spiritual moment was a defining event that shaped the rest of my life.

God's love. It is the very foundation for the book of Malachi. God sends His prophet to say some hard things to His stubborn people, but He leaves no doubt that His discipline flows from His heart of love.

Further Study and Reflection:
ADDITIONAL SCRIPTURES:
John 3:16-17   Psalm 13:5
Psalm 118   Isaiah 38:17

QUESTIONS TO PONDER
1. What was one of your all-time favorite gifts to receive as a child?

2. What does this chapter tell you about the love of God?

3. Who first told you that "God loves you?" How did you respond?

4. How have you seen the love of God at work in your life?

CHAPTER TWO

EXPRESSING YOUR LOVE TO GOD

MALACHI 1:6-14

"A son honors his father, and a servant respects his master. I am your father and master, but where are the honor and respect I deserve?"
Malachi 1:6 NLT

Is there a junk drawer in your house? You know what I'm talking about. When you don't know where to put something – it gets tossed in the junk drawer. It might be in the kitchen, or in the laundry room. You might even have a junk drawer in every room of your house!

Some of you might actually know what's in your junk drawer. Or maybe you haven't emptied it in years, and have no idea what lurks inside. In either case, the junk drawer is probably in a state of disarray.

So, how does the junk drawer tie in with Malachi? The prophet repeatedly calls the Israelites to get their lives in order. He is entreating them to clean out the "junk drawers" of their hearts and lives.

During my years in ministry, I have often heard people use this excuse: "I will give my life to God as soon as I clean up my act." That's not the way it works. We don't clean up our lives – He does. When we give ourselves to Christ, He forgives and makes us new. We have a new life, and a new nature. But it doesn't happen instantly.

We can stubbornly hang onto certain areas of our lives—our junk drawers. (For some of us, entire rooms in our lives might be in disarray.) We know we need to get our lives in order, but the process scares us. What dirt will be uncovered when we open the drawer? Mercifully, God is not wagging His finger in condemnation about our junk drawers. When God exposes our junk, cleansing and freedom are the results, not guilt and shame.

God used the prophet Malachi to uncover the Israelite's junk. It hurts to have our hearts revealed. To prepare the people for his painful message, Malachi began with the foundation of God's love. We can trust the Lord with our junk drawers only after we have experienced His unconditional love.

As Malachi delves into the condition of the Israelite's

hearts, worship is item number one on the prophet's agenda:

> "A son honors his father, and a servant his master. If then I am the Father, where is My honor? And if I am a Master, where is My reverence?" says the Lord of hosts to you priests who despise My name. Yet you say, 'In what way have we despised Your name?' (Malachi 1:6)

> "But you profane it, in that you say, 'The table of the Lord is defiled; and its fruit, its food, is contemptible.' You also say, 'Oh, what a weariness!' And you sneer at it," says the Lord of hosts. "And you bring the stolen, the lame, and the sick; thus you bring an offering! Should I accept this from your hand?" says the Lord. (Malachi 1:12-13)

Worship is an expression of our love to God. But we can easily confuse worship with ritual. When we don't worship from the heart, we are just going through the motions. Suppose your spouse said, "Honey, I love you with all my heart!" But instead of gazing into your eyes, your sweetheart is staring blankly out the window. How would that make you feel? You'd wonder if their expression of love was sincere.

Malachi confronts this kind of lukewarm love in this section of chapter one. The people of Israel were not worshipping God from the heart.

CONFRONTING THE PROBLEM OF WORSHIP

True worship is expressed in the context of relationship. Malachi draws on three primary relationships with God – that of Father, Master, and King – to confront the problem of wayward worship in his day. In doing so, the prophet deals with three attitudes that must be corrected if we are to worship God in spirit and in truth.

DISRESPECT

The comedian Rodney Dangerfield is best known for his famous lament, "I get no respect." I wonder if he ever read Malachi 1:6, where God says, "Where is My honor?... Where is My reverence?" He is asking, "Where is the honor and respect that is due Me?"

Dangerfield might get a lot of chuckles, but God's question is no laughing matter. He is seeking reverence and respect. But sadly, He's not finding it, even among the people who are called by His name.

Early in our marriage, I had a lot to learn about respecting and honoring my wife. Take Christmas, for example. I thought that if I just bought her a gift, that would be a sufficient expression of my love for her. I fell into the bad habit of running out to the mall on Christmas Eve and finding a last-minute present for Joy. Sure, I gave her a gift, but I was not showing respect or consideration for her. I was just going through the motions; my heart wasn't in the offering.

One year, Joy decided that she'd had enough. She took me aside and said, "This Christmas, don't do what you did last year. Don't go out on Christmas Eve at 5 o'clock in the afternoon and grab whatever is left on the shelf. It makes me feel like I'm not important to you."

She then reinforced her point by saying, "The only things left on those store shelves by Christmas Eve are everyone else's rejects. By picking up a reject for me, you think that you are fulfilling an obligation."

My eyes were opened that day. I had disrespected our marriage. I wasn't expressing love to my wife; I was giving her the leftovers. My actions were thoughtless, not thoughtful. Convenience mattered more to me than her feelings. The message that I was sending to Joy certainly didn't sound like, "You are special to me."

If our relationship was going to grow and improve, I had to put my heart into it. I needed to value and respect Joy, and not just go through the motions.

Expressing Your Love to God... 29

According to Malachi, the people of God, then and today, are guilty of the same thing. We think it is sufficient if we just show up for worship. Hey, we've fulfilled our religious obligation for the week. We mouth the words to the songs without our hearts being fully engaged. This kind of disrespect can only negatively affect our relationship with God.

DESPISING ATTITUDES

After dealing with disrespect, Malachi points out a second attitude that needs correction. Verse six addresses, "To you priests who despise My name." The religious leaders of that day, the ones who should have known better, were targeted for this stinging rebuke.

You can hear the indignation in their response. "Yet you say, 'In what way have we despised Your name?'"

Malachi is quick to respond: "How have you despised the name of God? I'm glad you asked! You priests despise the Lord's name by what you call worship. Oh sure, you bring sacrifices. But instead of bringing the best you have to God, you give Him the worst. You've brought blind goats, and lame sheep—you've even offered Him carcasses of dead cows. And you dare to call this an expression of your love for God?"

The Old Testament law required that every offering brought to the Lord had to be perfect. Why? Fast-forward to the New Testament. We no longer offer animals for sacrifice, because Jesus is now the sacrifice for sin. The Old Testament sacrifices were a picture of the perfect sacrifice of Jesus, the Lamb of God, who was without spot or blemish.

God required a perfect sacrifice. The Israelites knew this, but they still violated His command. They insulted God when they brought their lame, stolen, and dying animals as an offering to Him. Malachi exposes their hypocrisy when he asks,

"And when you offer the blind as a sacrifice, is it not evil? And when you offer the lame and sick, is it not evil?

> *Offer it then to your governor! Would he be pleased with you? Would he accept you favorably?" says the Lord of hosts. (Malachi 1:8)*

Most of us probably don't regard the IRS with warm affection. God points out that His people regarded their own government more highly than they did Him. Can you image that?

Suppose your income tax is due on April 15th, and you write the IRS the following letter:

Dear Friends,

At our house this past year, we've run into a streak of bad luck. Our children have been sick. I've missed a number of days at work and lost some much-needed income. Therefore, we won't be able to send our income tax this year. But I've included the title to my old, broken-down car. It's not that we don't care. We really do. But we have other responsibilities.

Your friend,

Joe Citizen

Now, what do you think the IRS is going to do with that letter? Are they going to say, "Well, isn't that nice? His words and intentions are good enough, he doesn't have to give anything this year"? Not likely.

But people come to God and say, "I know the tithe is holy unto You, but Lord, we've had a streak of bad luck recently in our lives. Would You mind getting the stale leftovers?"

The people of Israel were eating their cake, and giving God the crumbs. The prophet cuts across this nonsense and says, "What's wrong with this picture? You have despised the Lord. You honor your earthly authorities over your God."

It is sacrilegious to say, "We love you, Lord. We'll give You the stuff we don't want." This expression of sacrifice is not sacrificial at all. Their expression of "love" cost them absolutely nothing.

DEFILING ACTIONS

Malachi next identifies a third problem area—defiling actions.

Malachi 1:13 reads, "You also say 'Oh, what a weariness!' And you sneer at it," says the Lord of hosts."

Notice the downward spiral depicted in the verses we've examined. What starts as a bad attitude ends up as an action that offends God. The Israelite's defiled sacrifices and stinking carcasses were a stench to their own priests, yet they expected God to look the other way. The picture would almost be comical if it weren't so ludicrous: the children of God had to plug their noses while they worshiped!

I know people who come to church and feel like they have done God some huge favor just by showing up. These folks will sing, if the music moves them. They often sleep through the prayer. They scope out the lobby after church for any new business contacts. If there are any mistakes in the bulletin, they'll notice. Rather than take sermon notes, they critique the message. They check out what sister Wanda is wearing and what brother Walt is driving. These people can hardly wait for the service to end, but as they are driving home, they pat themselves on the back for doing their Christian duty.

The zeal for worship has faded. The risen Christ speaks to this very issue in the book of Revelation. He rebukes the church in Ephesus by saying, "You have left your first love." (Revelation 2:4)

Our attitudes affect our actions. A disrespecting and despising attitude will eventually result in defiling and disobedient actions. When our love for God grows cold, it gets easier to disobey Him. Jesus put it this way in John 14:15, "If you love Me, keep My commandments." If you are having a difficult time obeying the Lord, work on your love relationship. The obedience flows naturally out of love.

Today, we don't offer up diseased animals to God when our love grows cold. We defile God's altar occurs when we willfully disobey Him and refuse to repent of our sins. Hebrews 10 identifies this problem:

> For if we sin willfully after we have received the knowledge of the truth, there no longer remains a sacrifice for sins, but a certain fearful expectation of judgment, and fiery indignation which will devour the adversaries. Anyone who has rejected Moses' law dies without mercy on the testimony of two or three witnesses. Of how much worse punishment do you suppose will he be thought worthy who has trampled the Son of God underfoot, counted the blood of the covenant by which he was sanctified a common thing, and insulted the Spirit of grace? (Hebrews 10:26-29)

This passage states that when you know the right thing to do, and choose to disobey anyway, you are treating the blood of Jesus as an unholy thing. There is fearful judgment attached to this kind of disobedience.

CORRECTING THE PRACTICE OF WORSHIP

The prophet doesn't just point out the Israelite's failures in worship. He offers them solutions. For every reproof that Malachi gives, he presents a remedy. He lays out three positive principles that will correct the problems outlined above. By incorporating these principles, we, too, can restore worship to its rightful place as the center of our lives.

REMEMBER THE NATURE OF GOD

The word "worship" means "to attribute worth." It describes our response to God's worth. To remedy an attitude of disrespect, we must remember the nature of God. People who don't enter into worship don't know God. They may envision Him as a cosmic cop, or a senile grandfather. Or, they might perceive Him as distant and impersonal.

But Malachi reveals God's nature in verse six: "If I am the Father, where is My honor?"

God is not an impersonal force; He is our father. He is

intensely personal. However, God is not to be confused with our earthly fathers. Some might say, "If God is anything like my dad, thanks, but no thanks." In the Lord's prayer, Jesus identified God as, "Our Father in heaven." He is personal, He is a father, but He is a perfect Father in heaven. He has no failings, unlike our earthly fathers. As a father, God deserves honor. We are to respect Him as our Father in heaven.

When my children were very young, Joy and I lived in a small house on the church property. You could see the church office from our house, which was across the parking lot.

About five o'clock every afternoon, I would make the short journey from the office to our home. My children would be looking out the kitchen window, anticipating my return. Joy would proclaim, "Here he comes!" and out the door they bolted, across the porch, down through the lawn, past the hedge, and into the parking lot.

"Daddy! Daddy! Daddy!" they would shout in unison, their arms outstretched, eager for my hugs and kisses. My work as a pastor was important, but this was the highlight of every day. It was the kind of moment that you wish you could freeze and put on hold for the rest of your life.

There is a powerful bond between my children and me because they know me as their daddy. The same connection happens spiritually when we acknowledge God as our Father. This is the essence of worship. Something powerful happens when God's children gather together and acknowledge Him as "Abba (Daddy), Father." Our hearts are connected with His. We are at home with Him.

We are God's children, but we are also His servants. Verse six continues, "And if I am a Master, where is My reverence?" This takes the relationship to another dimension. God is the master; we are the servants. It's not the other way around.

In Malachi's time, slaves were sold at auction to the highest bidder. As our Master, the Lord has purchased us. He paid the highest price —the life of His Son— in order to redeem us.

We belong to Him. 1 Corinthians 6 tells us that, "you are not your own, you were bought with a price."

God wasn't bargain shopping when He bought you. You weren't purchased at the discount store. He paid the ultimate price. This means that you are extremely valuable to God. When God says, "I am a Master", He is saying, "You are valuable to Me; so valuable that I purchased you with the life of My Son."

We are precious to God. But He is still the Master, and we are His servants. Our response to this Master of love is to serve and obey. Both the father-child and master-servant relationships operate on the principle of obedience. Obedience is simply respect and honor in action.

The apostles called themselves bond-servants, or slaves:

Romans 1:1—"Paul, a bond-servant of Christ Jesus, called as an apostle, set apart for the gospel of God . . ."

James 1:1—"James, a bond-servant of God and of the Lord Jesus Christ . . ."

2 Peter 1:1—"Simon Peter, a bond-servant and apostle of Jesus Christ . . ."

Jude 1:1—"Jude, a bond-servant of Jesus Christ, and brother of James . . ."

It is a high and holy calling to be a bond-servant of Almighty God!

REVERENCE THE NAME OF GOD

In verse six, the Lord accuses the priests of despising His name. These learned men were the spiritual role models of their day, and they were profaning the name of God. Profanity isn't just a dirty joke or a four-letter word. We can profane the name of the Lord when we stand together and sing about the holiness of God—but we're thinking about what we are having for lunch. If the words we sing are empty, and mean nothing in our hearts, we are as guilty of taking the name of the Lord in vain as if we had used His name as a curse word. It is irreverent.

God's name is worthy of reverence. By His name we are

saved, healed, protected, and delivered. If you sing, "I love you, Lord" and you mean it – that is true worship.

David, whom the Bible describes as a man after God's own heart, knew what it meant to be a worshipper. After he restored the Ark of the Covenant to the temple, David wrote in 1 Chronicles 16:29, "Give to the Lord the glory due His name. Bring an offering and come before Him. Oh, worship the Lord in the beauty of holiness!"

RECOGNIZE THE NOBILITY OF GOD

"For I am a great King," says the Lord of hosts, "And My name is to be feared among the nations." (Malachi 1:14)

God is our Father and our Master, but He is also our King. As Father, we are to honor Him. As Master, we are to serve Him. As King, we are to bow before Him and give Him homage.

God is not our cosmic grandfather, or our heavenly Santa Claus. He is the King of all kings. As the maximum authority in the universe, He is not an autocratic dictator, ready to punish us for every small mistake. He is history's only perfect and good and righteous king. He is royalty, and when we worship Him, we will never be in higher company.

Jesus taught more about the Kingdom of God than any other topic. It is supremely important that we learn how to live as subjects in the Kingdom, and it means, first of all, that we ascribe worth to our King.

TOOLS OF WORSHIP

There are rules for worship, but there are also tools for worship. Often when we think of tools for worship, we think of singing hymns or praise choruses to express our love to God. But worship extends far beyond music. Worship doesn't just happen during the music part of a church service. Worship should happen when you use the opportunities that life presents as tools for honoring and respecting God.

I like the story that illustrates the differences in our worship traditions. An old farmer went to the city one weekend and while he was there, he attended the big church in town. When he returned home, his wife asked him how it went. "Well," he replied, "it was good. They did something different than what we do at our church, though. They sang praise choruses instead of hymns."

"Praise choruses?" asked his wife. "What are praise choruses?"

"Oh, they're okay," he said, "they're sort of like hymns, only different."

"Well, what's the difference?" she wanted to know.

The farmer described it this way. "Well, it's like this. If I were to say to you, 'Martha, the cows are in the corn' – well, that would be a hymn. But if I was to say to you, 'Martha, Martha, Martha, Oh, Martha, Martha, Martha, the cows – the big cows, the small cows, the brown cows, the black cows, the white cows, the black and white cows, the cows, the cows, the cows – are in the corn, are in the corn, are in the corn!' Well, that would be a praise chorus!" said the farmer.

WORSHIP IN SPIRIT AND IN TRUTH

Worship extends far beyond music. You worship the Lord when you confess your sins to Him. When you sing, "Create in me a clean heart, O God, and renew a right spirit within me," you are singing David's confession of sin to God in Psalm 51, and the grace he experienced as a consequence of his repentance.

You worship the Lord when you fully trust Him. Proverbs 3:5 says, "Trust in the Lord with all your heart, and lean not on your own understanding." When you acknowledge, "God, you're bigger than anything that I have to face. I put my trust in You," you are worshipping the Lord.

You worship the Lord when you serve others. Jesus said in Matthew 25:40, "inasmuch as you did it (serve others) to one of the least of these My brethren, you did it to Me."

There are many other examples. You worship the Lord when you pray. You worship the Lord when you live by His word, when you obey Him. You worship the Lord when you love each other. You worship the Lord when you maintain a true and consistent witness. In every arena of life, we have opportunities to worship God.

Many centuries ago, two brick layers were working side-by-side. A passerby asked one of the men, "What are you doing?"

He replied, "I'm laying bricks. Day after day, I come to work and it's the same thing. It's back-breaking, boring work, laying bricks."

"Well, then, what are you doing?" the stranger asked the second man.

"Why, I'm building a great cathedral to the glory of God!" the other brick-layer exclaimed. These two men were doing the same thing, they but had entirely different attitudes. One was worshipping God through his work.

The heart of Malachi's message in the second half of chapter one is this: true worship is costly; it requires effort and obedience.

King David understood this principle. In 2 Samuel 24, the nation of Israel was suffering from a plague. David's first response was to worship the Lord in the midst of this trial.

As David searched for a suitable place to make a sacrifice, he met a landowner named Araunah. This man owned a threshing floor and had animals for sacrifice. When he saw King David coming, he ran and fell on his knees and said, "O great King! I am honored that you've come here."

"I have come to worship God." King David informed him.

"You can have my threshing floor," Araunah told his

king. "In addition, you can have any animals you want. You can have my properties. I'll give it to you at no cost."

If you want to learn something important about worship, study David's response. In 2 Samuel 24:24 David says, "No, but I will surely buy it from you for a price; nor I will not offer burnt offerings to the Lord my God with that which costs me nothing."

Malachi addressed a nation that had forgotten this principle. Jesus reinforces this teaching in His parable of the widow's mite. Luke 21:1-4 reads, "And He looked up and saw the rich putting their gifts into the treasury, and He saw also a certain poor widow putting in two mites. So He said, 'Truly I say to you that this poor widow has put in more than all; for all these out of their abundance have put in offerings for God, but she out of her poverty put in all the livelihood that she had.'"

Several years ago, over a thousand people filed into church to attend the funeral of Julee Meyers. Many who came that day were believers because of Julee's testimony. Before the funeral service concluded, more individuals had turned to Christ. The large crowd didn't assemble just to pay tribute to Julee. They were drawn together to celebrate the presence of God that permeated Julee's life.

Julee Meyers, an attractive blonde in her forties, had just lost a lengthy battle with brain cancer. Even in her last hours, however, she chose to be defined by her love for God rather than the disease. Her positive spirit affected everyone around her. Julee had been bed-ridden toward the end of her life, but it didn't limit her ministry. She even led people to Christ over the telephone.

Julee was a hero, but she suffered from discouraging moments just like we all do. Late one evening, Julee called me. Both she and her husband were feeling overwhelmed and oppressed. After five years of remission from her first bout with cancer, new tumors were detected. The doctors warned her that the cancer appeared to be more aggressive than before. Julee had been suffering from this relapse for several months, and she was weary. She needed a fresh touch from God to finish the race.

I drove to her home, praying all the way. I didn't have a magic wand to make her problem disappear. I didn't have a clue what to say. When I arrived, Julee confessed to me that worship had become a struggle for her. I suggested that we pray together, and she agreed.

We lifted our hearts to God and the atmosphere of the room changed. Darkness and depression vanished and joy poured in. The presence of God surrounded Julee as she chose to worship in the midst of the greatest battle of her life.

Julee's fight continued, but her heart had changed. Instead of giving in to discouragement and fear, Julee chose to praise God. She told me that she would sometimes feel the support of the angels as she literally walked through the valley of the shadow of death.

People who came to comfort Julee would leave encouraged themselves. She spoke life and truth to others, she lived in the Word, and she infected people with her love for God. I will never forget her attitude through these darkest of days—her tears of gratitude toward God for His love and His grace.

Julee wasn't healed of cancer, but she was transformed through worshipping God. Worship may not change our circumstances, but true worship always changes us.

Further Study and Reflection:
ADDITIONAL SCRIPTURES:
Deuteronomy 6:4-9   I Chronicles 16:29
Psalm 95:6   John 4:24   Romans 12:1

QUESTIONS TO PONDER:

1.   What are some of the ways you generally show a person you love them? (Give Attention - Acts of Service - Special Gift - Specific Words - Special Card – Other?)

2.   What is the main warning in this chapter in your opinion?

3.   What are some of the ways you can express your love to God?

4.   What advice would you give to a new believer regarding worship?

CHAPTER THREE

LEARNING TO ENJOY GOD'S BLESSING

MALACHI 2:1-6

"The purpose of my covenant...was to bring life and peace, and this is what I gave them."
Malachi 2:5 NLT

Have you ever been robbed? Maybe a thief broke into your home or stole your car. Perhaps a pickpocket lifted your wallet or nabbed your watch. Nowadays, even your identity can be stolen. The probability is high that you will be the victim of theft at some point in your life.

In 1992, I had the opportunity to take my family to the Dream Team Olympic Basketball game in Portland. We couldn't wait to see the best basketball players in the world all under one roof. I had just spent about $400 on our car before the event. The vehicle was ship-shape, with new tires and the works.

On the day of the game, we piled into the car and drove to the Memorial Coliseum, anxious to see the one-of-a-kind sporting event. What a wonderful evening we enjoyed together! After the game we headed toward the car. My son and I raced each other down the street to see who could reach it first. I beat him to the space where we had parked our Dodge Lancer, but the spot was empty. Our car was no longer there!

I just couldn't believe it. In shock, I walked back to my family and told them that our car had been stolen. At first they thought I was joking. But when I called a friend to come give us a ride home they knew this was the real deal.

Two days later, the police called to say they had found my car. I hitched a ride to the towing lot and paid $75 to retrieve it. The smashed-up wreck was barely recognizable, bearing little resemblance to the polished new car I'd parked on the street a few days earlier. I felt a sickening sense of loss.

Did you realize that we can be robbed spiritually as well as physically? The Bible describes Satan as a thief who comes to kill, steal, and destroy. Have the blessings that God intended for you to enjoy as a Christian been snatched from your life?

I have good news for you. The Lord can recover whatever Satan has stolen from our lives.

THE PROSPECT OF GOD'S BLESSING

God desires to restore blessing to our lives. That is His heart. But before we can experience God's goodness, we must be sure that we are not under God's judgment. This is the point of Malachi's rebuke. If we persist in sinning, we can't expect God to bless us.

> "And now, O priests, this commandment is for you. If you will not hear, and if you will not take it to heart, to give glory to My name," says the Lord of hosts, "I will send a curse upon you, and I will curse your blessings. Yes, I have cursed them already, because you do not take it to heart. Behold, I will rebuke your descendants and spread refuse on your faces, the refuse of your solemn feasts; and one will take you away with it. Then you shall know that I have sent this commandment to you, that My covenant with Levi may continue," says the Lord of hosts.'" (Malachi 2:1-4)

The priests were meant to be instruments of God's blessing to the people. But Malachi points out that the sinful actions of these spiritual leaders had hindered God's blessings. They had stirred up His wrath and invoked His judgment.

While Malachi's rebuke may seem excessively harsh, it is calling the priests to repentance—to change their wicked ways. God's heart is to restore His blessings to Israel and repentance is the key. It opens the door for forgiveness and restoration of relationship with God. Repentance always precedes revival.

While repentance may be humbling, it is not a negative thing. In fact, the results are always positive. It is a matter of perspective. Consider the time that Billy Graham was dining in the Senate cafeteria in Washington, D.C. A Senator stopped at his table and posed a question to the famous preacher.

"Mr. Graham," he said. "Several of us are having a debate about pessimism and optimism. Are you an optimist or a pessimist?"

"I'm an optimist," replied Billy Graham.

"And why do you say that?" the senator asked in surprise.

Billy Graham's answer was classic. "Because I've read the last chapter of the Book—and we win! That is why I'm an optimist."

Be an optimist as you read the book of Malachi. If the prophet's words sound negative or harsh, remember that God ultimately wants to bless His people. His heart is for restoration. He does not delight in rebuke, but He rebukes in order to correct and restore. The correction is for our benefit.

Malachi's words prepared the children of Israel for the first coming of Christ. As we read the book of Malachi today, our hearts are being readied for the second coming of Christ. Wrapped up in Malachi's rebuke are words of hope for the future.

THE PROMISE OF GOD'S BLESSING

> *"My covenant was with him, one of life and peace, and I gave them to him that he might fear Me; so he feared Me and was reverent before My name. The law of truth was in his mouth, and injustice was not found on his lips. He walked with Me in peace and equity and turned many away from iniquity" (Malachi 2:5-6)*

The promise of God's blessing is captured in one word that is repeated throughout chapter this chapter. It is the word "covenant." Notice how frequently the word is used in this passage:

Malachi 2:4 – "My covenant"
Malachi 2:5 – "My covenant"
Malachi 2:5 – "A covenant of life and peace"

Malachi 2:8 – "The covenant"
Malachi 2:10 – "The covenant"
Malachi 3:1 – "The messenger of the covenant"

Covenant is the main theme of this passage. Grasping the concept of covenant is essential to receiving God's blessing. If we are living within the parameters of the covenant relationship designed by God, the enemy cannot rip us off.

Understanding the covenant will equip you to enjoy God's blessing. As we look at the purpose of the covenant in this chapter, you will realize why Malachi is so upset at his fellow Israelites, especially the priests, for violating this covenant in their own hearts. Because their hearts were distant from God, their religious practices didn't amount to much more than just vain repetitions. The priests expected blessings from God, but because they had violated the covenant, they received curses instead.

THE MEANING OF COVENANT

What is a covenant? I live in a neighborhood that has covenants. For example, you cannot paint your house bright pink in our subdivision. Only certain colors are permitted. You cannot jack your car up, take off all the wheels, remove the transmission, and leave it more than 24 hours in your driveway. As a homeowner in this neighborhood, I have agreed to abide by these covenants.

When used in this sense, a covenant is a contract or an agreement on set standards. Merrill Unger, in Unger's Bible Dictionary defines a covenant as "a simple compact between individuals in which each party binds himself to fulfill certain conditions, and is promised certain advantages."

The biblical concept of covenant is much richer than a mere contract. It is a relational word. A biblical covenant formed a union between two persons or two partners. The covenant relationship made them partners in the most profound sense. They would mutually hold all of their assets together, including their talents, possessions, and even their liabilities. Covenant makers would often expand the terms to include their children in the partnership.

The term "covenant" actually comes from the word "to cut" and refers to the shedding of blood. The original Hebrew word is "B'rith" and means a blood covenant. It was a sacred agreement based on blood.

We've all heard of blood brothers. The Lone Ranger and Tonto are good examples of this kind of covenant relationship. In one of the first episodes, they cut their wrists and mingled their blood together. They were saying, in effect, "What's yours is mine. What's mine is yours. We will stand together, and if anybody ever comes to attack you, I will stand with you." They became covenant brothers, agreeing to stick together no matter what happened.

In biblical times, three distinct exchanges took place during a covenant ceremony. The participants pledged their person, possessions, and protection to each other. First, by mingling their blood, the parties were pledging their personhood. Their destinies would be intertwined one with another. Secondly, each person would remove his coat and offer it to the other. They were communicating, "Here are my possessions. What I have belongs to you." Thirdly, they often exchanged weapons (a bow or a sword) to symbolize the promise of protection.

The term "friend" comes from this covenant relationship. We use the word today to describe a casual acquaintance, but in the Bible, a friend was a covenant brother. The word implies unwavering commitment. Proverbs 18:24 says, "A man who has friends must himself be friendly, but there is a friend who sticks closer than a brother." This verse describes a blood covenant that went beyond family ties. A covenant brother sticks close to you, not because he is your relative, but because he made a solemn choice to be a part of your life.

The Bible refers to Abraham and Moses as friends of God (2 Chron. 20:7; James 2:23, Num. 12:8; Deut. 34:10). The Lord expressed His friendship with these two men through covenant relationship. Through the covenant ceremony, God and man pledged themselves to one another.

"Loving-kindness" is another covenant word that describes the quality of a covenant-brother relationship. It conveys the idea that "I am for you." A Psalm that is a familiar praise chorus is Psalm 63:3, "Thy loving-kindness is better than life."

Merrill Unger in his Bible Dictionary puts it this way, "Loving-kindness describes the attitude of God toward men and implies goodness, mercy, and grace extended at personal cost." It is not a passive sentiment, but an active expression of covenant relationship.

God reminds the priests in Malachi's day of His covenant with Levi, from whom the Levitical priesthood descended. That covenant was not obsolete, but was still operative. God still desired friendship with His people, and had a heart of loving-kindness toward them. He intended to bless those who would obey Him.

God had not forsaken the covenant—His people had. They had forgotten the sacred agreement their forefathers had made with God. And, in their negligence and disobedience, they forfeited the blessing.

Could we be in a similar scenario today? God has provided us with a blood covenant through the sacrifice of His Son, Jesus Christ. Like Malachi's original audience, we have the ability to forsake, forget, and forfeit the blessings that God intends for us to enjoy. Are we keeping up our end of the bargain?

YOUR PART IN THE COVENANT

Look at Malachi 2:5 once again, "My covenant was with him (Levi, the priest), one of life and peace, and I gave them to him that he might fear Me; so he feared Me and was reverent before My name."

What application does the Old Testament covenant have with a New Testament believer? Here's the deal. Today's Christian takes the place of the priests in the old covenant. Revelation 1:6 says, "And (He) has made us kings and priests..."

In the Old Testament, the priests were a special class of people, who stood between God and man and mediated the blessings of the covenant. But the New Testament teaches the priesthood of all believers. Thanks to the sacrifice of Jesus on the cross, we don't need a mediator. We all have direct access to the Father through the blood of the Lamb.

We must understand our position as "priests" to be able to enjoy God's riches and blessings. Christ paid the penalty of your sin with His blood. When you placed your faith in His saving work on the cross and received His grace, you became His child. Every child of God is also a priest in His kingdom. 1 Peter 2:9 says, "But you are a chosen generation, a royal priesthood, a holy nation, His own special people..."

Preachers and theologians might try to complicate this issue, but the truth is quite simple. While it may be simple, it is not easy to live out. And Satan is always eager to try and steal this truth from our lives.

Some of us have been robbed of the blessing. Instead of counting our blessings, we end up listing our troubles. We see ourselves as victims, rather than victors. But when we understand who we are in Christ, we will no longer allow circumstances to dictate how we live our lives.

THE TERMS OF THE COVENANT: LIFE AND PEACE

God has made a blood covenant with you. He counts you as His friend. You are a member of His royal family, and you have direct access to Him twenty-four hours a day, seven days a week. The terms of the covenant are life and peace. These are the blessings of the covenant relationship that are stated in verse five.

The Bible teaches that God is life. This is the biblical

equivalent of a mathematical equation. Separation from God is death—relationship with God equals life. Jesus said in John 10:10, "The thief does not come except to steal, and to kill, and to destroy; I have come that they may have life, and that they may have it more abundantly." The purpose to our existence, and the reason we were created, is to experience relationship with God, which is life.

Peace is the other blessing of the covenant mentioned here. It is a by-product of our relationship with God. We live in troubled times and if peace were a commodity that could be purchased, the price would be out of sight. But Jesus is the One who has purchased peace for us: "Therefore, having been justified by faith, we have peace with God through our Lord Jesus Christ" (Romans 5:1).

THE PICTURE OF GOD'S BLESSING

The friendship of David and Jonathan is famous for the depth of devotion between the two men. They came from opposite backgrounds—one grew up in a palace, the other in the country. Through divine circumstances, they met and became friends. God knit their hearts together and they entered into covenant relationship with each other.

Jonathan became a mighty warrior in his father's army. There weren't any cell-phones or computers in those days, so David could only admire his friend from a distance. But the two had a heart connect that carried them through times of separation. Before Jonathan had gone into battle, he had given David his robe and his sword. The gifts spoke of covenant relationship—"In person, in possession, and in protection, I will stand with you."

David also proved to be a mighty warrior. But his success roused King Saul's jealousy, and a price was put on David's head. David became a fugitive, separated from his beloved Jonathan until the tragic day of his friend's death.

In one terrible battle, the lives of both King Saul and Jonathan were ended. David succeeded Saul as King of Israel, and all who were left in Saul's family fled for their lives. David didn't know it at the time, but there was still a legal heir to Saul's throne—the son of Jonathan, his covenant friend.

When David took the throne, the royal nurse packed up the child and fled into the wilderness. In her panic, she tripped and fell on the little boy, breaking both of his legs. She bandaged him the best she could, and continued on her desperate journey.

As the child grew, his legs became twisted and malformed. He couldn't walk without help. In that culture, such a weakness was despised. So Mephibosheth lived in the wilderness, physically crippled and broken in spirit, apart from the blessing that should have been his.

David, however, never forgot his covenant friendship with Jonathan. One day he asked this question: "Is there anyone still left of the house of Saul to whom I can show kindness for Jonathan's sake?" One of his servants remembered Jonathan's son. And he knew where to find him.

King David sent an entourage of royal guards and chariots into the desert to find Mephibosheth. When the young man spotted the king's entourage heading his way, he was terrified. Mephibosheth thought, "This is it. My life is over. They've finally found me." All of his life, he's been told that the king was his enemy, and because his grandfather Saul had hated David, that David hated his family and would retaliate for past grievances.

When Mephisbosheth was brought before King David, he fell to the floor in terror. But David quickly dispelled his fear with the joyful proclamation: "Your father, Jonathan, was my covenant brother and friend. I have been looking for you in order to bless you." Mephibosheth expected the worst, but was offered blessing beyond his wildest imagination.

Before Mephibosheth could speak, David continued, "I'm showing you this kindness because your father and I had a

Learning to Enjoy God's Blessing... 53

blood covenant. We made an agreement. What was his was mine, and what was mine was his. I want to include you in this covenant, but it's up to you." Jonathan's son had a decision to make. He had to change his mind about King David and realize that he wasn't the enemy. He had to choose to receive the blessings.

On that day, Mephibosheth changed his mind and chose the blessing. Just hours before, his future seemed bleak, but his life changed forever because of the covenant his father had made with the King.

David kept his oath of friendship. He expressed lovingkindness to Mephibosheth and offered him the blessings of life and peace. Imagine the contrast! He had awakened that morning in the wilderness, now here he was in a warm palace. Yesterday he'd sat down at a makeshift table and eaten crumbs. Today he would feast at the King's banquet. These blessings were his because King David had said, "Today, Mephibosheth, I want you to be my son."

I imagine that Mephibosheth witnessed many reminders of his father as he lived in the King's palace. The scar on David's wrist was a reminder of the blood covenant he had made with his father. Perhaps he put on Jonathan's robe, which David still owned and cherished. No doubt Jonathan's sword and bow were displayed in a prominent place as a testimony to their friendship and their pledge of protection to each other.

The story of David and Mephibosheth is a picture of the blessing that God intends for you. God is not your enemy. He wants you to be His child, and He wants to bless you with life and peace.

THE PROVISION OF GOD'S BLESSING

The story of Mephibosheth applies to us all. We have been crippled and deformed by the fall. We have been dethroned by Satan's lies. Living outside of covenant relationship is akin to living in the wilderness. But the King, through a blood covenant, has offered us a reprieve. He gives us a chance to share in His royalty. The Father is calling us to come home.

A covenant is an agreement made between two persons based on blood. That is the message of the cross. It is man's blood mixed with God's blood. Jesus was both human and divine. He fulfilled both sides of the covenant. He was both God and man, making a new covenant for us to live under and enjoy. Jesus Himself put it this way - "This cup is the new covenant in My blood, which is shed for you" (Luke 22:20).

As a result of this blood covenant, we enjoy and experience four specific blessings from God.

Blessing #1: **Forgiveness.** By dying on the cross, Jesus offers forgiveness of sins. You can be free from guilt and shame. You can be free from negative, destructive habits that control you. Jesus offers total cleansing, and a clean slate, regardless of your past.

Blessing #2: **Fellowship.** You can have a relationship with Almighty God! You can be connected to Him, and know that He is watching over you at all times. He desires friendship with you, and He will never leave you or forsake you.

Blessing #3: **Fortune.** Philippians 4:19 says, "And my God shall supply all your need according to His riches in glory by Christ Jesus." Through Jesus, our every need will be supplied. All of the resources of heaven are available to us. We are heirs of God and joint heirs with Jesus Christ.

Blessing #4: **Family.** You can be connected to the family of God. You don't have to be lonely or face life's trials by yourself. You are no longer an outsider looking in, you are part of a family. As 1 John 3:1 says, "Behold what manner of love the Father has bestowed on us, that we should be called children of God!"

Hosea 4:6 says, "My people are destroyed for lack of knowledge." Like Mephibosheth, many people live in despair because they don't know the truth. They think God is their enemy; they don't know that God is for them. They are ignorant about their rights and privileges as a child of God.

You can be sure that Satan doesn't want you to know about God's covenant. He wants you to be a beggar. He delights to see you bound by depression and guilt and failure. The devil's goal is to keep you in the wilderness and out of the palace.

"You're not worth anything," he'll whisper in your ear. "You're not valuable to God. He is not on your side. After all you've done, how could He bless you? You're a loser."   As the accuser of the brethren, Satan is an expert at suppressing the truth.

But if we know that we are heirs of God and priests in His kingdom, we can just point to Christ's sacrifice, the blood covenant, and say, "I don't have to listen to you anymore, Satan. All that stuff may be true, but it is time for me to go to the palace, where I belong."

Further Study and Reflection

ADDITIONAL SCRIPTURES
  Psalm 103:1-5   Mark 11:24   John 3:15   John 6:35

QUESTIONS TO PONDER

1. Have you ever been robbed? What took place and how did you feel?

2. Why did God speak so strongly to the Priests?

3. How would you describe a Covenant according to this chapter?

4. What impact has God's Covenant had on you?

CHAPTER FOUR

MARRIAGE: PULLING TOGETHER WHEN YOU ARE PULLING APART

MALACHI 2:10-16

"And this is the second thing you do: you cover the altar of the Lord with tears, with weeping and crying; so He does not regard the offering anymore, nor receive it with goodwill from your hands. Yet you say, 'For what reason?' Because the Lord has been witness between you and the wife of your youth, with whom you have dealt treacherously; yet she is your companion and your wife by covenant. But did He not make them one, having a remnant of the Spirit? And why one? He seeks godly offspring. Therefore take heed to your spirit, and let none deal treacherously with the wife of his youth. For the Lord God of Israel says that He hates divorce, for it covers one's garment with violence," says the Lord of hosts. "Therefore take heed to your spirit, that you do not deal treacherously." (Malachi 2:13-16)

Perhaps you've heard the story about the man who was involved in a serious car accident. When he regained consciousness, he was lying in the arms of his wife. She gazed at him with tenderness and concern. Her touch brought strength. The injured man could barely talk, but he managed a few simple words.

"Honey," he whispered, "you've always been there for me. You were there when I lost my job. You were there when I fell off the ladder and broke my arm. You were there when I went to the hospital for surgery and had my appendix removed. Now, here you are again for me."

Then he paused. His loving wife stroked his cheek and asked, "Yes dear, what else?"

"Well," he said, "I've decided that you are bad luck!"

The relationship we call marriage has many rewards, but also many challenges and adjustments. For many of us, marriage is where the rubber meets the road when it comes to living out our faith. Most of us will be married at one point in our lives, and Malachi's words on the subject reinforce his theme of getting our lives in order.

Things haven't changed much since Malachi's time. There really is nothing new under the sun. Marriages and families were disintegrating in the nation of Israel. It was fashionable in some circles to trade in first wives for new-and-improved pagan models.

God cares deeply about the marriage relationship. It is the foundation of the family and society. Stable families produce a stable community. But when the family structure is crumbling, the problem will manifest itself in social breakdown.

Take, for instance, the three most common problems among youth today: poverty, illiteracy, and crime. According to studies, the main contributing factor for all of these social problems is absentee fathers. When the marriage bond is forsaken, all of society suffers.

The influence of our marriages lasts far beyond our lifetime. Malachi will refer to the "godly seed" which is the result of a godly marriage. Marriage is more than the union of two people – it is the spiritual foundation for the future of society.

THE SERIOUS ISSUE PRESENTED: MARRIAGES PULLING APART

"Therefore take heed to your spirit, and let none deal treacherously with the wife of your youth." (Malachi 2:15)

"Who Wants to Marry a Millionaire" premiered on the Fox network in February 2001. During the program, scores of women competed for the bizarre prize—the opportunity to wed a wealthy bachelor. One lucky lady prevailed, and the two strangers were joined in "holy matrimony" at the end of the show.

Their relationship didn't have a chance. The happy couple didn't even make it through the honeymoon. Their prime time marriage was over even before it started.

What a sad commentary on our culture. That evening, millions of viewers witnessed a disposable marriage; a throwaway relationship. The God-ordained union was trivialized and demeaned. A more recent second show, called "The Bachelor" will no doubt have the eventual same result.

Marriage had been cheapened to a similar degree in Malachi's day. God's people, rather than influencing the surrounding culture, were being influenced by it. They were buying into the immoral and destructive values of their day, and leaving a string of broken families and lives in their wake.

None of this escaped God's notice. In His love and grace, God sent Malachi to warn His people about the emotional and spiritual consequences of divorce. God knew the lasting spiritual implications of broken marriages, and wanted to spare the next generation from devastation.

In his book, What America Believes, George Barna writes that one in four marriages in America ended in divorce during the nineties. You would think that with all of the conveniences we have in this country, all of the marriage counseling that is available, and all of the churches we have to choose from, fewer marriages would end in divorce. But we still choose to dispose of our spouses at a higher rate than most third world countries. Even more disturbing is the statistic that the divorce rate in the church is now higher than it is in the world.

While marriages may be falling apart in staggering numbers, God's heart is to pull families back together. He specializes in restoring broken relationships and hearts.

One of my closest Christian friends experienced the pain of divorce many years ago. I asked him, "If you had the opportunity to speak to people about divorce, what would you say?" Tears came to his eyes and he said, "I wouldn't hold anything back. I would try to convey the sense of pain that comes with divorce, and I would try to communicate a spirit of redemption."

My friend echoed Malachi's timeless message concerning marriage.

BROKEN DOWN FAITH

Several years ago I was driving down the freeway in the slow lane. In front of me was a huge, expensive motor home. As I got closer, I noted that it had a bumper sticker that said, "We spent our kids inheritance on this."

I thought to myself, "Those poor children."

I moved into the left lane of the freeway to pass, and realized that the motor home was being towed. As I got closer, I saw that the entire engine compartment had burned up

That is such a picture of what has happened for so many people who have wasted their kids inheritance, I thought as I passed the useless vehicle. *All that remains is an expensive piece of broken down equipment that is going nowhere.*

That motor home is like a lot of marriages—the burned-out engine compartment is like our faith. A marriage may look good on the outside, but without faith it is going nowhere.

Throughout this passage, Malachi emphasizes the interconnection of faith and marriage. Do you notice the word he uses repeatedly?

Verse 10 – "Why do we deal treacherously with one another?"

Verse 11 – "Judah has dealt treacherously"

Verse 14 – "You have dealt treacherously"

Verse 15 – "Let none deal treacherously with the wife of his youth"

Verse 16 – "Do not deal treacherously"

The underlying concept of treachery is treason. One translation describes this word as "breaking faith." These people had violated God's covenant of marriage. Recall that a covenant was a solemn pledge of unconditional commitment to another person. Living within the parameters of the covenant was the key to receiving the blessings of God. By violating the marriage covenant, the Israelites had broken faith with God. His blessing had been removed and they were going nowhere.

Malachi rebuked the Israelites severely for breaking their covenant with the Lord. Verse 12 says, "May the Lord cut off from the tents of Jacob the man who does this...yet who brings an offering to the Lord of hosts!"

"Big deal!" you say. "Tents are for nomads. I don't need a tent!" But the "tents of Jacob" was a metaphor for the line of God's blessing. There is a correlation between breaking faith, and breaking the line of blessing. This verse says that if a believer has broken faith with his wife (and consequently - with God), that God is not going to honor his sacrifices or his offerings.

God doesn't care about status. But He does care deeply about His covenant. In today's terms, this means that even if a man is a church member, even if he brings tithes and offerings to the Lord, even if raises his hands in worship—he will be cut off from God's blessings if he is unfaithful to the wife that God gave him.

When it comes to marriage, God doesn't have a return policy. He expects His people to express their faith by keeping the marriage covenant. He wants us to be blessed. He wants our children to be blessed. He wants the community to be blessed through healthy families.

That is why, in verse 16, God says emphatically, "I hate divorce." Listen carefully to what it does *not* say. God does not say, "I hate divorced people." God hates divorce because of its terrible impact on the people He loves.

WHY DOES GOD HATE DIVORCE?
First, it disobeys the Word of God

The concept of divorce doesn't exist in traditional wedding vows. "Until death do us part," is the promise made. The minister, quoting from the words of Jesus in Mark 10:9 will then say at the conclusion of the service, "What God has joined together, let no man separate." This is a clear declaration of God's intent. From the beginning, God's intent for marriage did not include divorce.

Second, it diminishes the worship of God

The marriage altar, a place of beauty, had become a place of shame. Yet the Israelites presumed to come and worship at that very altar. Malachi confronted their hypocrisy: "You cover the altar of the Lord with tears, with weeping and crying, so He does not regard the offering anymore" (verse 13). God was not moved by their tears and their offering. Because they had broken the marriage covenant, their worship was an abomination to God. They had "profaned the Lord's holy institution which He loves" (verse 11).

A little background; a look behind the scenes, will be helpful here. The Hebrew men at that time usually married young girls. When the beauty of youth began to fade, these men would sometimes "trade" their aging wives in for a younger model. Hebrew women could be divorced for burning the toast, or any other petty reason a dissatisfied husband could think of. After divorcing their Jewish wives, the men would often take pagan brides. And still they dared to come to the altar to "worship" God!

Third, it destroys the work of God
But did He not make them one, having a remnant of the Spirit? (Malachi 3:15)

It is a great mystery, but God is present in the union of husband and wife. Marriage is not man-made, but was God's idea in the first place. In Genesis 2:18, God declares, "It is not good that man should be alone." This was the first negative note in the creation account. We were created for relationship, not isolation.

The Apostle Paul, quoting from the Genesis narrative, writes in Ephesians 5:31, "For this reason a man shall leave his father and mother and be joined to his wife, and the two shall become one flesh." Total dynamic oneness – a sharing of body, soul, and spirit. This is God's intent for marriage.

But another purpose of marriage is to portray our relationship with God. Paul continues in Ephesians 5:32, "This is a great mystery, but I speak concerning Christ and the church." The marriage relationship reflects the very nature of God. There is relationship in the Godhead. Father, Son, and Holy Spirit have relationship with one another. Even though they have separate and distinct personalities, they are one. Likewise, husband and wife (who have a remnant of this same Spirit) are one.

Becoming one reflects the nature of God, and divorce destroys His handiwork.

Fourth, it distorts the witness of God
> *And why one? He seeks godly offspring. (Malachi 3:15)*

God desires our marriages to last because He seeks godly offspring. There is no question about what is best for the children. A mother and a father who are committed to God and to each other—that is God's prescription for healthy children.

As devastating as divorce can be for adults, children are the ones who are hurt the most. Children suffer physically, emotionally, and spiritually from the break-up of marriages. Kids pay a high price for their parent's selfish and sinful choices. Unless their hurt is addressed and healed, these kids often enter into unhealthy relationships and repeat the mistakes of their parents.

Parents have a unique opportunity to impact the world through their children. The offspring of a godly marriage offer light and hope to our sin-sick culture. God knew that the monotheistic Hebrew culture could be wiped out in a few generations if the marriage covenant was forsaken.

THE ROAD TO RECOVERY

I will never forget (though I'd like to) the evening I sat on the front row at a testimonial service. People took turns sharing with the congregation what God had been doing in their lives. One woman grabbed the microphone and announced to her fellow believers, "I'm so happy tonight. God told me to divorce my husband. Hallelujah!"

I thought to myself, *I don't think that was God, lady.* She was listening to the wrong voice.

"Well," you say, "doesn't God want me to be happy?" Have you heard that before? It's a FAQ (frequently asked question) that reflects cultural Christianity more than biblical Christianity.

God does want His children to be happy, and there are statements to that effect in the book of Malachi. But holiness is more important to God than happiness. Happiness is not meant to be the goal of our lives, but is rather, a by-product of right relationship.

If you set out on the road to happiness, you will never get there. But if you set out on the road to holiness, you will find happiness along the way. Jesus put it like this: "Whoever seeks to save his life will lose it, and whoever loses his life will preserve it" (Luke 17:33).

God wants you to be holy and in right relationship with Him. Holiness is the place to begin on the road to recovery.

Another FAQ is "Does the Bible permit divorce?" Yes, God allows for divorce for two reasons in Scripture. The first reason is adultery (Matthew 19:9); the second is abandonment (1 Corinthians 7:15). But even in those instances, the Bible doesn't say that you *must* divorce because of those things. In such cases, the Word allows a person the freedom to divorce, but it is not mandatory. God always encourages reconciliation and recovery.

We have a nickname for tow trucks in America; we call them wreckers. But when I was in Britain, I noticed that the tow trucks there have one big word written on the front, as well as on the doors – it is the word "recovery." When I saw that, I thought, *Here is the same vehicle, with the same equipment and the same mission, yet two totally different perspectives.* We say, "There goes a wrecker." But in Great Britain, they say, "There goes a recovery." I vote for recovery, how about you?

We are likewise presented with two perspectives on marriage: wreckage or recovery. I vote for recovery and redemption.

I want every follower of Christ to have a breakthrough, not a breakdown. In my experience as a pastor, I have witnessed the miraculous recovery of marriages that I thought were headed for the scrap yard.

One particular couple comes to mind. They had been married for seven difficult years and had young children. Money had become a source of contention between the two and they had separated. Divorce papers were eventually filed, and both husband and wife spent thousands of dollars on attorney's fees fighting each other.

People in our church prayed for this couple. They received support and counsel. Just when it seemed that there was no chance of this relationship ever being restored, God began to do a mighty work in their lives. The hopeless situation changed when they humbled themselves and began to take responsibility for their own mistakes and their personal relationship with Christ.

As long as God is in the equation, there is hope. Rather than wrecking our marriages, we must work toward recovery.

THE SCRIPTURAL INSIGHT PROVIDED: OF MARRIAGES PULLING TOGETHER

But did He not make them one, having a remnant of the Spirit? (Malachi 2:15)

God's arithmetic doesn't seem to add up at times. He says, "One plus one equals one." One husband plus one wife equals one flesh. Jesus affirms this truth when He quotes from Genesis 2:24: "For this reason a man shall leave his father and mother and be joined to his wife, and the two shall become one flesh." (Mark 10:7)

There are three concepts to note in this passage. First, consider the word "leave." The term refers to establishing the priorities of marriage. Before marriage, blood relatives took priority. After the wedding, the spouse comes first.

Men are then commanded to leave their parents. While this refers to physical distance, it also deals with emotional attachment. The man must transfer his allegiance from his parents to his wife—he must "cut the apron strings." Ideally, both husband and wife enter into the marriage relationship as independent adults, no longer emotionally dependent on mom and dad.

Secondly, a man is told to "be joined to his wife." The King James Version translates the word joined as "cleave" (not cleaver – that's divorce). Cleaving depicts the permanency of marriage. The marriage relationship is meant to be an indissoluble union. The Hebrew text suggests being glued together, like super-glue.

Finally, "the two shall become one flesh." The marriage is consummated in body, soul, and spirit. "One flesh" refers to more than just the physical expression of sex. It is a picture of the ultimate communion between two people.

The marriage relationship has supreme importance in God's scheme of things. It is more important than your business, your friends, or your church attendance. It's more important than your investments or your reputation.

Our culture, even the Christian sub-culture, has a difficult time swallowing this truth. So many people are coming from broken homes, where there was no intimacy or affection. At best, these families just co-existed under the same roof. At worst, they suffered abuse. Marriage, as God intended, has not been a reality in their lives.

FOUR BIBLICAL COMPONENTS OF MARRIAGE

1. STRONG COMMITMENT

Therefore take heed to your spirit, and let none deal treacherously with the wife of his youth. (Malachi 2:15)

Another translation of this verse says, "Do not break

faith with the wife of your youth." This speaks of commitment.

Unyielding commitment causes marriages to flourish. When a couple comes to the altar, they are making a commitment before friends, family, and God. They are making a sacred covenant. The marriage that is rooted in commitment to God has a better chance of enduring.

Believe it or not, there are times when my wife does not like me. There are times when I don't like myself! But we made a commitment to each other, promising that we will stay together. In our relationship, divorce is not an option. In fact, we never even say the "D" word because that would interject it as a possibility in our thinking. (We've mentioned murder on a few occasions, but not divorce!) The gold rings we wear daily remind us of the unending commitment we made to each other.

If you are spiritually single—and by that I mean you are married, but not to a Christian spouse—God honors your commitment in your marriage. 1 Corinthians 7:14 says, "For the unbelieving husband is sanctified by the wife, and the unbelieving wife is sanctified by the husband." In other words, you cannot use the excuse that your spouse is not a believer to abandon the marriage. It may be difficult to be "unequally yoked," but the Christian spouse always has the opportunity to be a godly witness to the unsaved partner. God's will is for us to use those opportunities, not lose them.

Ecclesiastes 4:12 says, "A threefold cord is not quickly broken." It takes three to make an unbreakable marriage. That third strand is the presence of God, and it is a key ingredient to a strong marriage. I cannot love my wife the way God loves her, at least not over the long haul. I can try for awhile, but I am not consistent. But when I invite God into our marriage, I can love my wife with His love. When God is the center of a marriage, there is no challenge too difficult.

We live in a day of "no-fault divorce." But I have to tell you, I've never encountered a no-fault divorce in my years of ministry. Someone is always at fault – usually both parties are to blame, at least to some extent. Divorce has become an easy way out—or at least so it seems.

But God calls us to long-term commitments with Him and our spouses. Commitment is a choice, not a feeling. It grieves Him that we bail out of covenant relationships when hard times come. He never intended for us to push the escape lever of divorce when we don't get our way. (I told Joy that if she ever leaves me, I'm going with her!)

Even the best of marriages go through stormy times. Why do some couples divorce while others stay together? It is commitment that keeps marriages together during the turbulent seasons of life. This commitment doesn't happen by accident, but is intentional. It is not based on feeling, but it is based on faith. Judith Viorst puts it well when she writes, "The best thing about marriage is that, when you fall out of love, it keeps you together until you fall back in love."

2. SPIRITUAL CLEANSING

"For the Lord God of Israel says that He hates divorce, for it covers one's garment with violence," says the Lord of hosts. (Malachi 2:16)

Notice the word "violence" that is used here. This refers to an attitude, not a specific action. It exposes a hard attitude toward a marriage partner – the wife, in particular. (Women were not even considered persons under the law in those days, with no legal rights or protection. Often, they were helpless victims in divorce.)

God says that divorce covers one's garment with violence. When a man would marry, in the Hebrew tradition, he would remove his outer garment in the ceremony. He would then take that garment and he would drape it around his wife. That was a covenant sign that symbolized spiritual commitment, emotional protection, and love.

Remember the story of Ruth? When Boaz promised to

marry Ruth, he covered her with his garment. It was a symbolic way of saying, "I am going to stand by you, and I will protect you and provide for your needs. I will take care of you for the rest of my life."

Malachi gets to the heart of the matter in this passage.

"Time out, guys. You have taken the coat off from the wife of your youth, and you have placed it on a woman who doesn't even believe in God. You have left your wife completely exposed and without protection and provision – and that is an act of violence."

What does that have to do with cleansing? The word "cover" is a metaphor for coming clean before God. It denotes hiding our sin—the opposite of transparency.

These Hebrew men who divorced their wives had left them uncovered and unprotected. This was bad enough. But when they placed the garment on that foreign woman in remarriage, the act of covering her was symbolic of trying to hide their sin before God.

Through Malachi, God is calling us to come clean before Him. Many marriages struggle because of unresolved baggage. Abuse, anger, lust – these are destructive patterns that can be covered up during courtship. After we say, "I do," these habits don't automatically get healed or go away. When the first crisis comes along, those old patterns often resurface.

When Joy and I were dating, she intentionally tried to upset me on a number of occasions. She knew how to push my buttons! Finally, I asked her why.

"I wanted to see what you were like when you were angry," she informed me. I'm glad I passed that test!

We all have struggles. And we need to come before the Lord on a regular basis and make sure that our hearts are right with Him. Is there anything hidden in your life that may someday trouble your marriage? I know women who had abortions years ago, but they still struggle with guilt. Smuggled into a marriage, that guilt will hinder intimacy. Cleansing from the past is important. Come clean before God.

Many people think that marriage will solve their problems. Marriage doesn't solve our problems – it reveals them. If we are wounded before the wedding, we will bring that hurt with us into marriage.

You don't have to be perfect in order to get married. But you need to bring your issues and problems to God and let Him cleanse you and change you. The Lord wants to heal the brokenness in your life before you enter a committed relationship. This will better equip you to keep the marriage covenant.

Troubled marriages don't mend overnight. But if you are in this place, you can decide today to invite the grace of God into your relationship. "I acknowledged my sin to You, and my iniquity I have not hidden. I said, 'I will confess my transgressions to the Lord,' and You forgave the iniquity of my sin" (Psalm 32:5).

Believe and apply God's promises to your life. King David committed adultery with Bathsheba. To cover his sin, David had her husband murdered. The prophet Nathan confronted the King, and to his credit, David repented. Psalm 51 is the account of David coming clean before the Lord for the sins of adultery and murder. Verses 1-3 say, "Have mercy upon me, O God, according to Your loving kindness; according to the multitude of Your tender mercies, blot out my transgressions. Wash me thoroughly from my iniquity, and cleanse me from my sin. For I acknowledge my transgressions, and my sin is always before me." Verse 7 continues, "Purge me with hyssop, and I shall be clean; wash me and I shall be whiter than snow."

Hebrews 9:14 states, "how much more shall the blood of Christ, who through the eternal Spirit offered Himself without spot to God, cleanse your conscience from dead works to serve the living God?" Some of you may think that God could never forgive you—that you are beyond hope and redemption. But by means of the blood of Christ, God cleanses and forgives all who come to Him.

3. SUPPORTIVE COMMUNICATION

Zig Ziglar tells the story of a lady who sought her pastor for counseling. She was going through a divorce. The pastor asked her, "Do you have any grounds?"

"Oh yes," she said. "Nine acres, just south of town."

He said, "No, no, no. I mean, do you have a grudge?"

"No," she replied matter-of-factly. "We don't have one of those, but we do have a barn."

"What I mean is," said the pastor, who was exasperated by now, "Does your husband beat you up?"

"Oh no. I'm usually the first one up in the morning," she said. "I'm kind of a morning person."

He asked her one last question. "Then why are you having trouble with your husband?"

"Well," she said, "He just doesn't communicate!"

Marriages that last practice supportive communication. Marriage counselors state that sixty percent of divorces are due to a lack of communication between husband and wife. Did you catch that? Poor communication is the leading cause of divorce, according to these counselors.

The Bible gives us a lavish picture of communication in the Song of Solomon. Here is an entire book that is devoted to two lovers who become husband and wife. Sixty percent of the language in this book is the interchange between two married lovers. Throughout the book, husband and wife communicate on the most intimate level. They are celebrating their relationship.

I have heard that husbands and wives who have been married more than ten years have only about 37 minutes of conversation a week. That reminds me of the guy who said, "My wife says I don't listen to her. At least, that's what I think she said." It is vital to the health of our marriages to make time for communication.

Wives often complain that their husbands talked a lot when they were dating, but clammed up after the wedding.

These marriages may excel in other areas. The couples may be committed and have experienced God's cleansing power. But they don't communicate.

It's not just about speaking to each other. I know couples who exchange words— but most of their speech is destructive. Communication needs to be supportive. Paul writes in 1 Thessalonians 5:11, "Therefore comfort each other and edify one another . . ." The NIV translates this verse, "Therefore encourage one another and build each other up." What if you were to practice giving at least two compliments a day to your spouse? How do you think that would change the temperature of your marriage?

People often give me positive feedback after I preach a sermon. I enjoy the compliments, but there is one person that I wait to hear from more than anyone else. Her name is Joy.

I know that I'm pathetic, but sometimes I follow her around the house on Monday just waiting for her to say, "You did great!" I'll even bait her, and go fishing for compliments. I am seeking her support.

Joy and I have learned that we need to be each other's biggest fans. The only person whose opinion really matters to me is my wife. She is for me, and she lets me know it. One sincere compliment from her carries more weight than from everybody else combined.

Every marriage needs this powerful gift. Encouraging words are like waters flowing over dry, parched ground. The seeds of marriage will blossom and grow as we speak life to each other.

4. SHOWING CONSIDERATION

I meet many couples who are critical and argumentative. They are not kind to each other. Do you show consideration to your spouse by simple acts of kindness? Ephesians 5:33 says, "Let each one of you in particular so love his own wife as himself, and let the wife see that she respects her husband." Practice putting your spouse first. Recognize the value in each other.

Ruth Graham once said, "It's my job to love Billy Graham. It's God's job to change him." If you are trying to change somebody—especially your mate—stop it! Give that job to God and then commit to pray for that person. Prayer is a much more effective agent for change than criticism.

You can bring glory to God through your relationships. God is looking for men and women who will face their generation with courage and say with Joshua, "As for me and my house, we will serve the Lord" (Joshua 24:15).

We don't have to guess how God feels about divorce. God hates divorce, but He does not hate divorcees. He loves and restores them. Christ died for sinners, of which I am one. And if He came to save people, it seems to me that He has come to save marriages that are in trouble as well.

Divorce is not the unforgivable sin, and the church must remember that. Those who have been divorced are not second class citizens in the kingdom of God. If you've been divorced, come to Christ, and let Him begin a new work in you. Isaiah 1:18 reads, "Come now, and let us reason together," says the Lord. "Though your sins are like scarlet, they shall be as white as snow. Though they are red like crimson, they shall be as wool."

If you are married, or plan to be married someday, put Christ at the head of your home. If you are thinking of getting a divorce, think again. Get before God, and let Him do a work in your heart. You may never change the person you are married to, but God can change you. It might surprise you what God could do in your marriage if you will come to Him and let Him do His work in you.

Let our lives be a testimony of God's grace, and may our families be strong in the body of Christ. The greatest legacy we can leave to the next generation is a loving home where God is glorified.

Further Study and Reflection:

ADDITIONAL SCRIPTURES:
    Genesis 2:24   Proverbs 18:22   Matthew 5:32
    Mark 10:9   I Corinthians 7:3   Hebrews 13:4
    I Peter 3:1—7

QUESTIONS TO PONDER

1. Write down the name of a couple who has been a role model of a healthy marriage, in your life. What is it about their marriage that is special? What things do they have that you would like in your marriage?

2. How would you explain the statement, "God hates divorce," to someone?

3. What are some steps you would suggest to a person who has experienced the pain of divorce?

4. What advice would you give a young couple who came to you regarding building a healthy marriage and family?

CHAPTER FIVE

THE REFINING FIRE OF GOD

MALACHI 3:1-4

*"Who will be able to stand and face him when he appears?
For he will be like a blazing fire that refines metal..."*
Malachi 3:2 NLT

A first grade teacher collected several well-known proverbs and asked her students to complete them. She gave her class the first half of the common saying, and asked the students to finish them. The results were a reflection of the world from the eyes of a first grader.

*Better safe than...*punch a fifth grader.
*Strike while the...*bug is close.
*Don't bite the hand that...*looks dirty.
*Never underestimate the power of...*termites.
*A penny saved is...*not much money.
*If at first you don't succeed...*get new batteries.
*Laugh and the world laughs with you; cry and...*you'll have to blow your nose.
*Children should be seen and not...*spanked and grounded.

Well, that's what the kids thought these well-known phrases should say. They had their own ideas, and their answers made perfect sense to them.

But what about your life? How should your story be completed? Thus far, you have only the first phrase, and now you're trying to figure out how the rest of it should go.

The teachings of Malachi present us with "the rest of the story." We may have our own ideas that make perfect sense to us, but they don't compare to the timeless wisdom of God. Sometimes we try to put a period where God has placed a comma, or we attempt to fill in the blank with something different than what His loving hand has prescribed.

Malachi helps us take stock of what really matters as we go through the refining fire of God in our lives. He gives us a glimpse at the finished product. In order to see it, however, we have to shift from superficial living to supernatural living. That touch of the supernatural is the refining fire of God, which transforms and changes us.

The people of Malachi's day were "going through the motions" spiritually. They held to a form of religion, but they did not know the power of God. The same could be said of many church-goers today.

Such lukewarm spirituality may be commonplace, but it is far less than what God intends for His people. We settle for the superficial, when He offers us the supernatural. Malachi confronted the Jewish people with their shallow form of religion. He urged them to go deeper with God.

God didn't want their sacrifices and offerings. He desired something more; it was their heart condition He cared about. God wanted His children's hearts to be pure and their lives to be holy. The Biblical truth is this: it is not the offering that makes the worshipper acceptable; it is the worshipper that makes the offering acceptable.

THE PRACTICAL TRANSFORMATION OF YOUR LIFE
"For He is like a refiner's fire..." (Malachi 3:2)

Several years ago, I learned the hard way that my teaching ministry had become very shallow. A small group of college students came to my home and challenged me to take them deeper. They were hungry to grow in the Lord. But, they informed me, my teaching wasn't feeding them.

There are times in our lives where we find ourselves wading in ankle-deep water. It is comfortable. It is familiar. It cools us off a bit, but it's a superficial experience. These college students wanted to "take the plunge," and they challenged me to take my studies, my prayer time, and my teaching to a deeper level.

Recently, a friend came to me and said, "I am at a point in my life where I want to move from shallowness to significance." I knew what he meant. He was a successful and accomplished businessman, but he still felt that something was missing.

"I am full of myself, and I want to be full of God," he finally concluded. It was a breakthrough for him. Breakthrough day for us happens when we realize that we cannot do anything on our own, but we must rely on God.

Jesus began the Sermon on the Mount by making this foundational statement, "Blessed are the poor in spirit, for theirs is the kingdom of heaven" (Matthew 5:3). One translation puts it, "Blessed are those who have come to the end of themselves." Blessed are those who know their own spiritual poverty.

Declaring spiritual bankruptcy is difficult and painful. It runs contrary to our flesh. Whether someone else points out your deficiency, or the Holy Spirit lets you know– it is humbling. But holiness begins with humility.

My friend's life changed dramatically that day. I have seen God at work through this man's wise and godly decisions in his business. He approaches God everyday with an expectant heart, trusting that the Lord will use every situation to take him deeper. The challenges he faces have not changed, but his approach to the challenges has changed him.

How will you experience transformation in your life? Where will you begin? It's easy to say that we're going to change. But when push comes to shove, change forces us out of our comfort zone. Even if our lives are superficial, there is security in what we know.

In chapter 3, Malachi exhorts us to submit to God's refining fire. The Lord wants to burn away the dross and remove the impurities from our lives. We must remain moldable and malleable as God purges our hearts. We will feel the heat, but the finished product will reflect the character of Jesus Christ.

I have found that there are four elements that are essential to becoming more like Christ. The first step begins with accepting the grace of God. It all begins with God's grace.

1. RECEIVE THE GRACE OF GOD

"Behold, I will send My messenger, and he will prepare the way before Me.
And the Lord, whom you seek, will suddenly come to His temple, even the
Messenger of the covenant in whom you delight.
Behold, He is coming," says
the Lord of hosts. (Malachi 3:1)

Look at the opening phrase of verse 1 - "I will send My messenger, and he will prepare the way the way before Me." This is a prophetic reference to John the Baptist. He was the forerunner who prepared the way for Jesus. He announced the coming of the Messiah.

Verse 1 continues, "And the Lord, whom you seek, will suddenly come to His temple." In the Old Testament, God had a physical structure – the temple for His people. But in the New Testament, God has a people who are for His temple. Paul put it this way in 1 Corinthians 6:19, "Your body is the temple of the Holy Spirit." He went on to say, "You are not your own. For you were bought at a price; therefore glorify God in your body and in your spirit, which are God's." You are designed to be a dwelling place for God.

To move from the superficial to the supernatural, we need the grace of God in our lives. A supernatural walk begins with God when we let our bodies—our temples—be the habitation of the Holy Spirit.

When you give your life to Christ, you receive the forgiveness of sin. Not because you deserve it; not because you are a good person and all your neighbors love you; not because you put money in the offering plate and sing in the choir. You receive forgiveness – that's the grace of God.

When you receive God's grace, you experience His presence in your life. The Holy Spirit takes up residence when we ask Christ into our hearts. In the Old Covenant, God lived in a physical building, which was the temple. In the New Covenant, He lives in the physical bodies of believers.

God Himself looked forward to this New Covenant:

> "Behold, the days are coming," says the Lord, "when I will make a new covenant with the house of Israel and with the house of Judah – not according to the covenant that I made with their fathers in the day that I took them by the hand to lead them out of the land of Egypt, My covenant which they broke, though I was a husband to them," says the Lord. "But this is the covenant that I will make with the house of Israel after those days," says the Lord; "I will put My law in their minds, and write it on their hearts; and I will be their God, and they shall be My people. No more shall every man teach his neighbor, and every man his brother, saying, 'Know the Lord,' for they all shall know Me, from the least of them to the greatest of them," says the Lord. "For I will forgive their iniquity, and their sin I will remember no more." (Jeremiah 31:31-34)

That, my friends, is the grace of God. This new covenant that Malachi refers to isn't the 11th Commandment, carved in stone. It is a new thing; God is writing it on our minds and our hearts. The new covenant recorded in the book of Jeremiah is the grace of God.

Every sin, every failure is forgiven. You don't have to lie awake at night, haunted by memories and the ghosts of guilt because those sins will be gone forever.

A counselor can help you manage your guilt, but only God can remove it and wipe the slate clean. Our guilt is what we rightly feel when we transgress against a holy God. But the blood of Christ cleanses us and sets us free. The work of the cross covers our guilt. Period. It is taken care of, and dealt with once and for all.

Don't settle for the superficial and the shallow. It may be comfortable, but it is not fulfilling. Settle for nothing less than a life of significance, substance, and supernatural meaning. It begins with accepting the grace of God.

2. RECOGNIZE THE GOAL OF GOD

> *But who can endure the day of His coming? And who can stand when He appears? For He is like a refiner's fire and like launderers' soap. (Malachi 3:2)*

The second step toward spiritual transformation is to recognize the goal of God. God has one purpose in mind for our lives, and that is to make us more like Jesus Christ. His grace accepts us just as we are. However, He loves us too much to let us remain that way. He refuses to leave us as He found us—lost in our sin.

Recently, I had the opportunity to go to a Hot Rod show. I'm a car guy – I appreciate vintage autos. At the show, I saw plenty of before-and-after photos of the cars. It was fascinating to see how they looked before restoration. Some had been on blocks, forgotten in a back yard. Others had broken down and had been discarded in a garage or a barn. They were wrecked, rusty, and worthless. But after having been lovingly and meticulously repaired, rebuilt, and repainted – they were in superb condition. These vehicles were showpieces.

As I looked at those cars, I thought, *This is what God is doing in my life. His refining fire in my life means that His loving hand is at work, welding, sanding, buffing, and remaking me to be ready for the showroom of heaven.*

He has taken us off the blocks, and is getting us ready for the palace. That process involves refining, renewing, and rebuilding. God isn't just restoring us to mint condition—we'll be better than new. When we get to heaven, we will see the before-and- after pictures, and they will be a testimony to God's grace.

I met Kevin at a men's retreat fourteen years ago. Kevin seemed so totally out of place that I wondered why he'd come. A construction worker, Kevin was pretty rough around the edges. He'd come out of a background of drug and alcohol abuse. Even though he was a believer, Kevin wandered aimlessly through life.

But at the retreat, God began to work in Kevin. I could almost see the Holy Spirit hammering out the rough spots - sanding, polishing, and remaking this man into a radiant picture of God's grace.

After the Lord got hold of him, Kevin got married. He went on to become a lead actor in our church's passion play, and then got active in missions. He shares what God has done in his life everywhere he goes.

Kevin has the joy of the Lord like few Christians I've known. Even his appearance has dramatically changed. People love to be around him. What a contrast to the first time I met him, when he was so out of place. But Kevin had a spiritual hunger and submitted to God's refining process in his life.

Psalm 66:10 says, "For You, O God, have tested us; You have refined us as silver is refined." Silver is a metal ore, which means that the raw material typically contains less than 1 percent silver and 99 percent everything else. These impurities are what need to be removed through a process that involves sifting and melting.

Crushing, sifting, and heat purify the silver. We throw broken things away, but God does not use anything until it is broken. God loves broken things and He redeems them to His use. Refining silver begins with the breaking process. The ore is crushed and ground into a fine powder and then sifted before it is subjected to the heat.

When we first come to Christ, we are like the ore. God sees only the faintest glimmer in us, but He knows it is there. Through his refining process, He patiently removes the impurities to obtain the silver.

Silver is used to make mirrors. A mirror has one purpose - to reflect an accurate image. God will not leave you how He found you. He has one goal in mind for your life – that your life would be an accurate reflection of Him.

3. REST IN THE GOODNESS OF GOD

He will sit as a refiner and a purifier of silver.
(Malachi 3:3)

The third step in the refining process involves waiting. When the refining fire gets turned up, it's easy to wonder, "Does God really love me?" That is the time to rest and abide in the goodness of God. We must wait for Him to take us out of the furnace in His perfect timing.

In verse 3, God is pictured as passive. He is sitting. But He's not just sitting around; it is purposeful activity. Our waiting and our enduring have purpose, too.

God will not walk away and abandon the project. He is not in it for the short term. Refining is a lengthy process. It takes time to melt the ore; then it takes time for the dross to rise to the surface so it can be scooped away. It takes time for the purification process to be completed.

I've had those times when the furnace is on and my life feels like it is melting all around me. I want to yell, "God, get me out of here! Are You listening? God, where are You?" The truth is that God is sitting right next to me, watching the process. God is part of the process. He is the refiner, and He stokes the fire. I don't like it a bit, but it is absolutely necessary for God to complete His work in me.

God turned up the heat in our family when our son Phil was 14 years old. My wife began to notice that sometimes Philip didn't respond normally at the dinner table. Right in the middle of a conversation, Philip would stop and just stare into space. We took him to a specialist, who determined that Phil was having slight, momentary seizures.

Philip began taking medication, and Joy and I began to watch and pray. The cause of his seizures remained a mystery until after he graduated from college. At that time, the seizure activity increased. A scan revealed that a tumor was growing at the base of Philip's brain. Surgery to remove the tumor was scheduled—just weeks before the date of Philip's wedding.

I don't need to tell you that the time prior to the surgery was a stressful period in our family's life. As traumatic and draining as that time was, however, we learned to rest in the goodness of God. His peace sustained us. Today, we thank God that the surgery was a success and there have been no further seizures.

I believe that there are three kinds of people: those being tested, those coming out of a test, and those preparing to have a test. Our response to the tests of life makes all the difference. If God's goal is to transform our character, then it is imperative that we pass the test. Endure the process and rest in God's goodness. Trust Him, because His intentions for you are good. The trials in your life are accomplishing something. The superficial is being replaced by the supernatural, the shallow by the substantial.

4. REFLECT THE GLORY OF GOD

That they may offer to the Lord an offering in righteousness. Then the offering of Judah and Jerusalem will be pleasant to the Lord. (Malachi 3:3-4)

The silversmith knows that the refining process is complete and the silver is pure when he sees his reflection in the silver. The Master Refiner has achieved His purposes when you reflect His image. He knows exactly what it takes to form you into a masterpiece. After the dross is removed, He turns the heat down. Then He begins to mold and form you. Then, He polishes you until He sees the reflection of His own glory.

Silver is a beautiful metal, and it is also extremely useful. It has long been used in the making of fine jewelry. Because of its electron configuration, all visible light is reflected in its surface. This attribute makes silver the metal of choice for mirrors and photo processing. Silver also has the highest electrical conductivity of all metals and it is used extensively in batteries.

It is not coincidental that God compares His people to silver. Silver is not only beautiful, it is useful. God's people—in their purest form and highest function—reflect God's glory and conduct His power and grace.

God's transforming work can been experienced at all levels of life—from the extraordinary to the mundane. When you find yourself behind a mathematically challenged shopper in the express checkout line at the supermarket, how do you respond? Instead of blowing a fuse, ask God how to handle the situation. He will teach you how to respond with courtesy and patience. When you are patient, you reflect the glory of God.

Do you procrastinate? If you are tempted to say, "I'll get to it later," ask God what He requires. No doubt God will begin teaching you the art of perseverance. He will say, "Stay with it, child. I want to see My glory in your life."

If your marriage is rocky and divorce looks like the easiest way out, ask the Lord what He is trying to teach you. As you wait on Him, He will teach you the way of unconditional love. There is no greater way to reflect the character of God.

God is a refining fire. He wants to refine you so that you will reflect His glory. Are you prepared to turn your life from the superficial to the supernatural? Only by consenting to His refining fire can we fulfill God's purpose for our lives.

Further Study and Reflection:
ADDITIONAL SCRIPTURES:
Psalm 51:1-7 Jeremiah 18:1-4 Romans 12:1-2
I Corinthians 6:9-11   James 4:8   I John 3:3

QUESTIONS TO PONDER:
1. Where did you first commit to be a follower of Jesus Christ?

2. What was one noticeable change in your life after accepting Christ?

3. What is the significance to silver and gold in this section of Scripture?

4. What do you feel is God's main goal in refining you?

5. What is God working on in your life right now?

CHAPTER SIX

IT PAYS TO TITHE

MALACHI 3:6-12

"Bring all the tithes into the storehouse so there will be enough food in my temple. If you do," says the Lord Almighty, "I will open the windows of heaven for you. I will pour out a blessing so great you won't have enough room to take it in. Try it! Let me prove it to you!"
Malachi 3:10 NLT

Not long ago, my family and I had an adventure. Joy, my two daughters, and I took a ride in a helicopter. None of us had ever flown in a chopper before, and it didn't look that scary. As long as we were on the ground, I was fine.

We buckled up and listened to some brief instructions. Then the helicopter lifted off. The pilot, who looked to be too young to have a driver's license, said, "We're going to ascend to an altitude of between ten and twelve thousand feet." I thought to myself, "I don't remember reading that in the brochure." I honestly didn't know that we were going to climb so high in the sky – into the clouds, no less.

As I digested that bit of information, our pilot added nonchalantly, "We will experience some minor turbulence." Now, in my opinion, when you're at 10,000 feet, there is no such thing as minor turbulence. So, I braced myself for major turbulence.

To reassure myself, I asked this young pilot (who was getting younger every moment), how much experience he had flying helicopters. Since this was my first flight, I wanted to make sure it wasn't his! So I asked, "Jeff, how long have you been flying helicopters?" He glanced at his watch, which made me even more nervous.

"Oh, about five minutes," Jeff replied with all the confidence in the world. The look of terror on my face told him that wasn't the answer I'd been hoping to hear. Not wanting his passenger to have a heart attack, he told me the truth. Jeff had been flying helicopters for eleven years.

That knowledge helped some, but I have to confess that just standing up in a balcony makes me nervous. And here we were, headed toward the clouds. We couldn't see the ground, we couldn't see the heavens—for a while we couldn't see anything.

My mind was beginning to imagine all sorts of frightful things and then the view cleared up.

For the next 45 minutes, we stared out the windows, transfixed by the spectacular scenery. When we landed, I wanted to do it again! What an experience!

This adventure reminded me of the law of aerodynamics. I don't know the technical aspects of aerodynamics, but a few pilots have tried to explain to me how helicopters are able to fly. Because of the law of aerodynamics, heavy objects like helicopters are able to rise up far above the earth.

The law of aerodynamics supersedes the law of gravity. Personally, I'm grateful for gravity. I'm glad that my feet are planted on the ground, and that I'm not floating out in space, somewhere. But the law of gravity can be overcome by the law of aerodynamics.

Just as there are laws of physics that govern how the universe operates in the physical realm, so there are spiritual laws that govern how things operate in the spiritual realm. The book of Malachi reminders us of the spiritual laws that God has established to help us get our lives in order. In Malachi 3:6-13, the prophet addresses the subject of money and the spiritual principles that help us govern that area of our lives.

Money is a touchy subject. It is important to us—we all need the stuff to survive in this world. Money is also important to God. God doesn't need money, but it is mentioned a lot in the Bible. Money was a favorite topic of conversation for Jesus. His number one was the Kingdom of God, but number two was money. Why? Because it's so important to us and is such a big part of our lives.

In Psalm 50:12 God says, "If I were hungry, I would not tell you; for the world is Mine, and all its fullness." In other words, God doesn't need your money, because it all belongs to Him anyway.

God knows that a commitment that doesn't touch our wallet won't reach our hearts. In Malachi 3, God lays out His spiritual principles concerning money. He promises to open up the windows of heaven and pour out blessing on our lives—if we first give to Him. God wants to bless us, but cannot do so if we are holding tightly to the purse strings.

The Bible has much to say about finances. Of the 38 parables of Jesus, 16 have to do with money and possessions. There are 500 verses on faith in the Bible and 500 verses on prayer, but there are 2,000 verses on stewardship and wealth.

Besides you and God, there is a third special interest when it comes to money – the devil. Satan is interested in your money, because he wants to mire you in financial bondage. He wants you to live under the curse of debt. He'd like you to have more month than money in your life, more sweat than equity, and more worry than wealth. He wants you to miss the blessing of God in your life because he is a thief.

Satan wants to steal from you, but God desires to bless you. In this Malachi passage, God gives us the blueprint for opening the windows of heaven and receiving blessing into our lives. Do you want to be ripped off, or do you want to be blessed? It's time that we pulled up the shades and opened the windows of heaven.

THE SPIRITUAL PRINCIPLE

"For I am the Lord, I do not change; therefore you are not consumed, O sons of Jacob. Yet from the days of your fathers you have gone astray from My ordinances and have not kept them. Return to Me, and I will return to you," says the Lord of hosts. But you said, "In what way shall we return?"
(Malachi 3:6-7)

Money is not just a neutral medium of exchange. Jesus characterized Mammon (which is the Aramaic word for "wealth") as a rival deity that competes for our allegiance with God. There is a spiritual side to money, so we must deal with it according to spiritual principles. Returning to God is the first principle of financial freedom.

When you recognize that your priorities are off track, turn back to God. God says, "Return to Me, and I will return to you." This is foundational for what follows. God takes the first step by saying, "I want you back. When we stray from Him, He doesn't force us back into relationship. But God the Father is waiting with His arms outstretched.

Note the word "return". This text is directed toward God's people. Those who have never turned to God in the first place cannot return to Him. This message is to God's people who are in financial bondage.

And what is financial bondage? It is simply spending more money than you make. This destructive pattern affects both the rich and poor. You can diagnose this ailment in your own life by just opening up the checkbook. Are your credit cards maxed out? Instead of paying them off, do you just apply for more credit cards and run those up, too? Do you borrow money to pay off fixed expenses like taxes or insurance? Have you prayed to win the lottery so you can get out of debt? Do you argue with your spouse about money?

Conflicts over money are the leading cause of divorce in this country. (I heard about a perfect marriage, except for one simple flaw. He was fast on the deposit, and she was quicker on the draw.)

It's not just the poor who struggle with money. You can be rich and be a slave to your wealth. If you buy things you do not need, with money you do not have, to impress people you do not like, you are in financial bondage. When we try to find satisfaction, security, and self-worth in having money, then we are in financial bondage.

Finally, financial bondage can tempt us to cheat God. We don't give freely to Him because we want to escalate our standard of living.

Do you tithe? Do you give to God's work and God's servants generously? If the answer is "no", then you are in financial bondage. I often hear people say, "But I can't afford to tithe." And that's precisely the problem. If you're not tithing, then God's not blessing.

God's plan for you—and His church—is financial freedom. Even churches can get turned around when it comes to money. God doesn't want to enslave us; He wants to bless us. That is the place to begin in our thinking. His heart is to bless. Jesus was quite clear in describing God's nature when He taught in the Sermon on the Mount, "Or what man is there among you who, if his son asks for bread, will give him a stone? Or if he asks for a fish, will he give him a serpent? If you then, being evil, know how to give good gifts to your children, how much more will your Father who is in heaven give good things to those who ask Him!" (Matthew 7:9-11).

Through Malachi, God is speaking to a people who have made a commitment to Him, but have not followed through with their finances. As a result, these people find themselves far from God's intended blessing, and He is calling them back. He says, "Return to Me." Financial freedom comes by first returning to the Lord.

Jesus said in Matthew 6:33, "But seek first the kingdom of God and His righteousness, and all these things shall be added to you." "All these things" refer to our needs – food, clothing, shelter. The key is to first seek the kingdom of God. Make Him your number one priority. Return to the Lord.

THE PATTERN

> "Return to Me and I will return to you," says the Lord of hosts. "But you said, 'In what way shall we return?' Will a man rob God? Yet you have robbed Me! But you say, 'In what way have we robbed you?' In tithes and offerings. You are cursed with a curse, for you have robbed Me, even this whole nation. Bring all the tithes into the storehouse, that there may be food in My house. And try Me now in this," says the Lord of hosts. "If I will not

open for you the windows of heaven and pour out for you such blessing that there will not be room enough to receive it." (Malachi 3:7-10)

Financial bondage is a symptom of a spiritual problem. The real issue is trust. Do you trust God in the area of finances? He wants to bless you, but are you willing to do what it takes to receive the blessing? God has set forth a specific pattern for receiving His blessing. It is the pattern of tithes and offerings. This is the practical application of what it means to return to the Lord.

The Jews of Malachi's day asked, "How can we return to You?" God replied, "Stop robbing Me." Then they indignantly questioned, "How are we robbing You?"

It would be better to rob a bank than to rob God. (No, I'm not suggesting that you go out and rob a bank.) I heard about one guy who went to rob a bank. He scribbled out a note, and passed it across the counter to the teller. The note read, "This is a stick up. Give me all your money, and put it in a bag. This is a robbery." She scribbled a note back, "Straighten out your tie. Put on a big smile. Because your picture is being taken at this very moment."

God knows who's stealing from Him. He asks, "Will a man rob God? Yet you rob Me. But you ask, 'How do we rob you?' God answers "In tithes and offerings. You are under a curse – the entire nation – because you are robbing Me."

God then commands the Israelites to "Bring the whole tithe into the storehouse." In response to their obedience, He promises a blessing of staggering proportions: He will open the floodgates of heaven and pour out so much blessing that there will not be room to contain it!

Tithing is not an abstract theological truth, but is a practical and tangible step toward God. The pattern that God lays before us here is very practical. It will work tomorrow, it will work next week, and it will work next year. You get your life in order financially by tithing.

Let's define our terms. The word "tithe" means one-tenth, or ten percent. A tithe is ten percent of income, off the very top (before taxes), dedicated to God's work. A tithe is not two percent, a tithe is not five percent, a tithe is not eight percent, a tithe isn't even fifteen percent. The word means ten percent. Giving five percent is not tithing. It's like being a little bit pregnant. There's no such thing. Either you are or you're not. Either you're tithing or you're not. To give more than ten percent is to give special offerings to God.

The Bible doesn't portray tithing as a burden. But many Christians today view it as such. In Scripture, however, tithing is always connected to a blessing, not a burden. It is an expression of love and trust in God. When we tithe, we are saying, "Lord, I love You, I believe in You, and I am giving to You."

Leviticus 27:30 says, "And all the tithe of the land, whether of the seed of the land, or of the fruit of the tree, is the Lord's. It is holy to the Lord." The concept of stewardship teaches that everything we have belongs to God. But God lays special claim to the tithe. It belongs to Him and is holy.

ISN'T TITHING JUST AN OLD TESTAMENT PRACTICE?

At this point, many Christians raise the question: "Isn't tithing just an Old Testament practice under the Jewish law? The Jews were under that law, but I'm a New Testament follower of Christ. I have been liberated. I am under grace. Aren't we now free from the law?"

The practice of tithing was established before Moses ever received the law. Four hundred years prior to God giving the Ten Commandments on Mount Sinai, Abraham, the father of the Jewish race, tithed to the high priest Melchizedek (Genesis 13). Melchizedek is a mysterious figure, with no record of where he came from, or where he went. Hebrews 7 refers to Melchizedek as a foreshadowing of Jesus. Some scholars suggest that he is a theophany – a pre-incarnation of Jesus. Jacob likewise tithed hundreds of years before the time of Moses.

"But that's the Old Testament," you may be thinking, "what about the New Testament?" Consider Matthew 23:23. In this passage, Jesus gets in the face of the Pharisees. He says, "Woe to you, scribes and Pharisees, hypocrites! For you pay tithe of mint and anise and cummin, and have neglected the weightier matters of the law; justice and mercy and faith. These things you ought to have done, without leaving the others undone." Jesus tells the Pharisees that they should continue to tithe, but stop neglecting the other issues. Tithing, mercy, forgiveness, faithfulness and justice should all be practiced. They are all part of the Christian life. Tithing was practiced before the law, tithing was taught through the law, and tithing was encouraged after the law.

Paul says in Romans 3:31, "Do we make the law void through faith? Certainly not! On the contrary, we establish the law." We, who are under grace, don't nullify the law—we uphold it. We don't get into heaven by works, but through our good works God can and does bring heaven down to earth. This is what Malachi 3:10 promises. Upholding the law isn't just about meeting minimum requirements. For example, state law mandates that parents feed their children. Failure to do so constitutes neglect. Now, why do you feed your children? Is it because the law says you must? No, you feed your kids because you love them. When our children were born, we didn't even know there was a law that required us to feed them. When they cried, we not only fed them, but we loved them, held them, and raised them. The law was on the books, but our love not only fulfilled the law, it went above and beyond the law.

THE PLACE FOR TITHING

The pattern has been established. The Bible says we are to tithe. But where are we to give the tithe? Who is the recipient? Through Malachi, God commands the people to: "Bring all the tithes into the storehouse, that there may be food in My house."

Now, where (or what) is the storehouse? In Old Testament times, the storehouse was in the temple. Today, a storehouse is a place you would go to in an emergency. The local church is the contemporary equivalent. It is to be the place where people go in a crisis, whether it is a spiritual or a physical emergency.

In 1 Corinthians 16:2, Paul writes, "On the first day of the week, let each one of you lay something aside, storing as he may prosper, that there be no collections when I come." Sunday is the first day of the week, and on that day we are to come together and bring the tithe. On Sunday you bring God's tithe, to God's house, so God's work may be accomplished in God's way. That's the way it is to be done.

Tithing isn't something dreamed up by a church board somewhere. "Hey, how are we going to pay for the ministry of the church? I know – let's ask everybody to give 10 percent of their income and we'll call it the tithe." The tithe is God's idea, not man's. I came across an interesting study recently. This study revealed that if everyone in the church lived at the poverty level, and all of them tithed off their meager income – the income of the church would double! What a tragic commentary on the state of the church. Jesus said, "For where your treasure is, there will your heart be also" (Matthew 6:21). Could it be that we value money more than doing the will of God?

Years ago, there was a popular bumper sticker among Christian circles that read, "Honk if you love Jesus." I was in Southern California recently and saw a bumper sticker that added a new twist to the old slogan. It said: "Tithe if you love Jesus. Anybody can honk."

THE SURE PROMISES

> "And try Me now in this," says the Lord of hosts, "if I will not open for you the windows of heaven and pour out for you such a blessing that there will not be room

enough to receive it." (Malachi 3:10)

God encourages us to put Him to the test. Normally, it isn't a good idea to test the Lord, but in this passage, God invites us to test Him. It is okay to put the Lord to the test here because He made the promise, and the promise is sure. We sometimes get confused when we think that God's blessing comes only in the form of financial gain. God doesn't say that if we tithe, we will become wealthy in worldly things. That may happen. But don't make the mistake of only seeking God for material blessings. The most valuable blessings are spiritual in nature, and He specializes in these.

What kind of blessings can you expect to receive from God? In this passage of Scripture, I see three promises.

GOD WILL RENEW OUR FAITH

First of all, God promises to renew our faith. He will throw open the windows of heaven and pour out such a blessing that there won't be room enough to contain it. Another translation speaks of it as opening the floodgates of heaven. Like fresh water on parched ground, your spirit will be refreshed as you experience His blessing. When you tithe, you will see the real God doing real things on your behalf. What could be more renewing for your faith than to witness firsthand that God keeps His word?

GOD WILL REBUKE OUR FOES

"I will rebuke the devourer for your sakes, so that he will not destroy the fruit of your ground" (Malachi 3:11)

The NIV translates this verse, "I will prevent the pests from devouring your crops." A century ago, almost 90 percent of Americans lived in rural areas. Americans were farmers, or at least closely connected to the land. When I was growing up, my father was the pastor of a church in an agricultural community in California. Most the people in our church were farmers, and they understood from experience the promise of Malachi 3:11.

I remember one year when a pestilence attacked many of the orchards of our valley. We had a close friend in that congregation named Ray Silber. He loved God and tithed faithfully. During that terrible year, Ray drove around his crop and he prayed Malachi 3:11. He said, "God, I have been faithful to You. I have brought my tithe into the storehouse as You have commanded. And based on this Scripture, I know that You will protect my crop." And amazingly, all of the orchards around his home were destroyed by this pestilence, but his was not touched. It was a testimony to God's blessing.

We all have our foes and adversaries. For a farmer it may literally be pests, but this principle holds true if you are a doctor or a contractor, a nurse or a schoolteacher, a homemaker or a store manager. If you tithe, God promises to rebuke your foes. I have even seen God take enemies and turn them into friends.

GOD WILL RESTORE OUR FRUITFULNESS

"... nor shall the vine fail to bear fruit for you in the field," says the Lord of hosts. (Malachi 3:11)

God promises a fruitful life. Now, this isn't a get-rich-quick-scheme. But if you are faithful to tithe, He will be faithful to you. Your car will drive further, your clothes will wear longer, your shoes will wear longer, and you will be healthier. Psalm 37:25-26 echoes this promise: "I have been young, and now am old; yet I have not seen the righteous forsaken, nor his descendants begging bread. He is ever merciful, and lends; and his descendants are blessed."

No matter what your income is, you will be better off on 90% with God's blessing than trying to live on 100% or 125% (like many are trying to live) without God. It is better to make God your business partner than to go it alone. Whether you make millions of dollars a year, or ten dollars a week for household chores, the principle is the same. If you follow the instructions, something supernatural will happen in your life that could not happen otherwise.

Throughout many years of ministry and raising a family, I have witnessed the faithfulness of God. Whenever we experienced God's supernatural provision for us, I would say to the children, "Kids, it pays to tithe." The sooner we learn this principle, the better.

I remember my very first job. I made all of five dollars a day! I'm grateful that my dad sat me down and explained the importance of tithing. He set a pattern for my life from the beginning. Because I learned that principle as a young man, tithing has never been an issue in our household. Giving to God is a natural expression of our faith.

Further Study and Reflection:
ADDITIONAL SCRIPTURES:
Proverbs 3:9-10 Proverbs 11:25 Matthew 6:33
I Corinthians 16:2   II Corinthians 8:1-8
Philippians 4:19

QUESTIONS TO PONDER:
1. What was your first job?

2. What was the mistake Israel made regarding money?

3. What does the word "tithe" mean? How does it apply to our earnings?

4. What does God promise to those who faithfully tithe?

5. What adjustments do you need to make regarding the way you handle your money?

CHAPTER SEVEN

THE REWARDS OF SERVING JESUS

MALACHI 3:13-18

*"They will be my people," says the Lord Almighty.
"On the day when I act, they will be my own special treasure."*
Malachi 3: 17 NLT

Have you ever been rewarded for your actions? As a child, did your parents motivate you to do your chores by saying something like, "If you clean your room, you can go to your friend's house for the afternoon?" Or maybe you received a scholarship for hitting the books and applying yourself in your studies in school. Students undergo tremendous hardships in order to receive that Master's degree or that Doctorate degree. Rewards can be powerful motivators.

Maybe you were rewarded by a promotion for your extra effort at work. A friend of mine was recently awarded a free luxury vacation for his sales achievements by his employer. Another friend was voted "Coach of the Year" by his peers at the university where he worked.

I know of three young men in the Portland area who received a handsome reward for capturing an escaped felon. Their names and photographs were published in the newspaper, and they received financial compensation for their assistance. A local news station selected one of these heroes, treated him to a haircut, bought him a new suit of clothes, and even helped him find a job.

Some rewards are more intangible. It is rewarding to see your children take their first steps. You call everybody you're close to, email everyone in your address book, and write everybody else, letting them know that junior took a step for himself, as if he were the first one who had ever done it. But it is one of the rewards of parenting. You can say, "It was worth getting up early in the morning, getting up in the middle of the night, changing diapers. Now he can walk on his own." What a reward!

I played football in high school. I remember one difficult season when the temperature soared above 100 degrees everyday during practice. We had daily doubles - grueling practice sessions twice a day—despite the oppressive heat. The fun of football faded during that time. I seriously considered early retirement from my budding career. But I stuck with it. My teammates and I worked through the pain; we persevered and we won the league championship. We each got a trophy with our name on it. (I won't tell you what year it was, but I think the alphabet had been recently invented!) Every one of us on that team received a reward, and to a man, we agreed, "It was worth the effort. It was worth all the pain and sorrow and everything else we went through – the hits, the missed blocks, and all of that – to get the reward." Somewhere in my garage I still have that trophy; a reminder of that sweaty, significant season in my life.

Those who plan long and work hard toward a goal achieve a calculated reward. On the other hand, those who are caught in the middle of a difficult situation and choose to do the right thing might receive an uncalculated reward. Regardless of the circumstances, in the end, the achievers will communicate the same idea: "It was worth all the pain and effort."

The key to appreciating a reward is to recognize its value. This recognition does not always come naturally for a Christian. If someone were to ask you about the rewards of serving Jesus, what would you say? Are the rewards something you recognize and appreciate?

When times are hard, it's all too tempting to say, "What's the use? Why should I serve the Lord?" God's people have voiced that complaint for thousands of years. The last half of Malachi chapter three addresses this negative viewpoint.

MAN'S FLAWED PERSPECTIVE

> *"Your words have been harsh against Me," says the Lord, "yet you say, 'What have we spoken against You?' You have said, 'It is useless to serve God; what profit is it that we have kept His ordinance, and that we have*

walked as mourners before the Lord of hosts? So now we call the proud blessed, for those who do wickedness are raised up; they even tempt God and go free.'" (Malachi 3:13-15)

"What good does it do to serve the Lord?" This question is the heart of the issue in Malachi 3. The Jewish people were speaking against God. They were complaining about the Lord. In their hearts, they believed that serving God is futile; a waste of time. They were giving up on God and moving on to other things.

Many believers today struggle with these issues. You may get up on Sunday morning and wonder, "Why should I bother going to church? It's a waste of my time. Everybody else seems to be having fun doing their own thing." This is the conclusion the Israelites had drawn. They looked around and thought, "Just look at those who don't serve the Lord. They seem to be getting along just fine. In fact, some of them are having more fun than we are!" From their flawed human perspective, they called the proud "blessed" (v. 15). In their eyes, it seemed that the wicked were lifted up. These people tempted God and faced no consequences.

I struggled with this issue as a teenager. One day, I told my dad that I was not going to go to church any longer. This posed a problem, since my father was the pastor. I grew up in the church, but found myself questioning the value of my faith. I finally came to the conclusion that attending church simply wasn't fulfilling for me.

In his wisdom, my father didn't overreact. He sat me down and we had a heart-to-heart talk. My father outlined for me the benefits of being part of God's family. He recognized that in my immaturity, I couldn't recognize the rewards of serving the Lord.

Many immature believers share this flaw, which I call spiritual myopia, or near-sightedness. If you suffer from near-sightedness, you have trouble seeing things from a distance. Spiritual near-sightedness occurs when we can only see what is directly in front of us. We see our own trials and the apparent prosperity of the ungodly. We may possess sight, but we lack vision. We can't see down the road.

It's easy to fall into the trap of thinking that evildoers prosper and those who challenge God escape. But God's redemptive purpose goes beyond the here and now. In addition, He has a redemptive purpose in the very struggles that you face. He confronts us with our attitudes, because He wants us to grow.

God can confront us through a counselor, a pastor, or a friend. He will send someone who can speak the truth to us in love. We may find the message painful, but God will go to great lengths to keep us from falling away from Him. So it was with the Israelites. God loved His people so much that He sent them the prophet Malachi.

GOD'S FAITHFUL PROMISES

Then those who feared the Lord spoke to one another, and the Lord listened and heard them; so a book of remembrance was written before Him for those who fear the Lord and who meditate on His name. "They shall be Mine," says the Lord of hosts, "On the day that I make them My jewels. And I will spare them as a man spares his own son who serves him." Then you shall again discern between the righteous and the wicked, between one who serves God and one who does not serve Him. (Malachi 3:16-18)

I know a wonderful woman who is an encouragement to me. She has attended the church that I pastor for more than 50 years. She and her husband raised their children here. This woman sits in the same place every Sunday and always has a cheerful smile on her face. After the service is over, she meets me at the door, and says, "I know you're busy, honey, but come here." (My wife says it's okay if she calls me 'honey.') She grabs my coat and she looks at me and says, "You know, pastor, it's good to serve God!"

I just have to give her a hug – she's such a dear woman. She always has a Scripture or two that she's memorized, along with a word of encouragement.

I don't know about you, but I need people like that. People who remind me from time to time that it is rewarding to serve the Lord. I need people who have been down the road, and have experienced a few hits in life, but they're still smiling because they have learned that serving the Lord is worthwhile. They don't have a near-sighted perspective, but they look at life from an eternal vantage point.

There are three rewards that I want you grasp in this passage. Get this into your spirit, because the day will come when a battle will be waged in your mind. It may happen during the hectic years of raising a family, or when you approach mid-life, or during your retirement years. But sooner or later, you will be tempted to take the easy road and abandon ship. The thought will cross your mind, "Why should I even be connected to a local church? What use is it to serve God? Why should I use my gifts for the glory of God?"

In those times, you can correct your near-sightedness by focusing on three rewards that will motivate you to keep on keeping on. When the enemy whispers in your ear and says, "This is a waste of time. This is a waste of your talent. This is a waste of your money," you will be able to draw on the assurance of these rewards. You will be able to resist the enemy and say "No!" to him.

REWARD #1:
THE ASSURANCE THAT JESUS REMEMBERS HIS OWN

Then those who feared the Lord spoke to one another, and the Lord listened and heard them; so a book of remembrance was written before Him for those who fear the Lord and who meditate on His name. (Malachi 3:16)

The first reward of serving Jesus is the assurance that He always remembers His own. The ones serving the Lord are identified in verse 16 as "those who fear the Lord." A vivid contrast is pictured here. While one group was saying, "It's not worth it to serve God, there is another group – a faithful remnant. This group got together, talked with each other, and encouraged one another. The most exciting part of this picture is how the Lord responds to this gathering. He took great delight in His faithful servants.

It's the same feeling that a father might have while watching his son stand up for the truth, or acting bravely when he doesn't even know dad is watching. It's as if God were saying, "That's my boy!"

I felt this way as I watched our daughter, Christy, minister to Katherine, one of her closest college friends. Christy and Katherine did everything together. Following graduation from college, Katherine returned to the east coast and made plans to be married. Christy flew from Seattle, Washington to Katherine's hometown to assist in the wedding and to serve as one of the bridesmaids. It was an exciting and emotional time for these close friends. But seven weeks after the wedding, the unthinkable happened. Katherine's husband was involved in a freak automobile accident. The young bride became a young widow before the honeymoon had ended.

Even though she was rocked with grief, Christy rose to the occasion. She emailed Katherine encouraging words and Scripture verses. With a maturity beyond her years, Christy ministered to her friend. When I read the things she wrote, and when I listened to what she said to Katherine, I wondered if I could have done as well. I watched God use Christy, and I saw her grow in wisdom and counsel. In the midst of a very dark time, I heard her say amazing things to her friends who were wrestling with this tragedy. I was so proud of her. I just wanted to say, "That's my girl!"

Throughout history, the Lord always has a remnant.

There has always been a group of people who believe that it is worth it all to serve God. Usually, it is just a small group, or band of disciples. But He has always had those who have decided to follow Jesus and not turn back.

Let me ask you, are you a part of that remnant, today? Are you one of those who have said, "I am going to follow the Lord, no matter what happens"? If so, there is the assurance that the Lord will not forget you.

If you are like me, you may feel at times as though God has forgotten you. We feel this way because we attribute human characteristics to God. Let me explain. Have you ever had the experience of being in a crowd of people with a close friend that you've known for years, and a new acquaintance comes up to you? Now, you remember this acquaintance's name, but you can't remember (for the life of you) the name of your old friend! You stand there and make small talk until his name comes to mind so you can introduce him. You've known him for years, and it's driving you crazy that you can't remember. I've been a pastor for over 20 years, and it is my business to remember the names of people I meet. But I sometimes forget because I possess the human characteristic of forgetting. People forget my name on a regular basis, too.

But here's the deal - God doesn't forget His people. Jesus said in John 10:27, "My sheep hear My voice, and I know them, and they follow Me." He is saying, "I know who My sheep are!" 1 Corinthians 8:3 affirms this same truth when Paul writes, "But if anyone loves God, this one is known by Him." In other words, those who say, "I'm going to follow God" are known by Him. This is a reward for serving the Lord. He knows who you are.

Take another look at verse 16. "Then those who feared the Lord spoke to one another. And the Lord listened and heard them. So a book of remembrance was written before Him for those who fear the Lord and who meditate on His name." Note the word "remembrance." A book of remembrance was written for those who belong to Him. This group had covenanted with one another to stand together for the Lord. This scroll of remembrance was precious to God. If you belong to the Lord, the Bible says that your name is written in the book of Life.

I once heard Dr. Adrian Rogers of the Bellevue Baptist Church in Memphis, Tennessee, deliver a message from Malachi 3:16. He pointed out that there are four things that God will remember about us and they are all mentioned in this verse.

1. Our Character. God will remember us for our character– whether or not we fear the Lord. I recently conducted a funeral for a dear friend of mine, Carl Rueck. He had been a member of the church for over 70 years. He died just short of his 94th birthday, but he was smart enough to know that a party up in heaven is far better than one down here. One day, I went to visit him at the care center. I held his hand and I heard him say, "I love Jesus." Those were the last words I ever heard him speak. Now, I don't know what you're going to say with your last breath. But that's what I want to say.

The word "fear" that's used in this verse has two primary uses in Scripture. It can mean "terror" or "respect", depending on the context. Those who don't know the Lord live in terror of Him. The Bible says that it is a fearful thing to fall into the hands of the living God. But those who belong to God don't live in terror – they live in respect and reverence of Him. If you don't know the Lord, then be afraid. If you know Him, however, terror is replaced by respect. It beats the alternative of being fearful.

Romans 3:18 says, "There is no fear of God before their eyes." This is how the apostle Paul, the author of Romans, sums up a grievous list of sins. Those who do not fear the Lord fall into sin. Godly character comes from knowing and reverencing God.

Proverbs 1 tells us that the fear of the Lord is the beginning of knowledge. A few chapters later, we read that the fear of the Lord is the beginning of wisdom. Knowledge and wisdom don't come from the classroom. They come from the fear of God. You can have a lot of data in your computer, but if you don't have a fear of God, it doesn't matter. It all begins with a knowledge of God, and a respect for the Lord.

2. Our Contemplation. Verse 16 speaks of those "who meditate on His name." Those who meditate on His name know that He is Jehovah Rophe, the Lord our Healer. They know Him as Jehovah Jireh, the Lord our Provider. They know Him as Jehovah Mekedish, the Lord our Righteousness. You say, "I don't feel very righteous or holy." Good. God is. So come to Him and let Him perform that in you.

If we meditate on His name, we come to know the Lord as Jehovah Rohi, the Lord our Shepherd. We experience Him as El Shaddai – God Almighty. We rejoice that He is Jehovah Nissi, the Lord our Banner. In the midst of our battles, we need His banner over us that declares: "I belong to God."

We get God's attention when we use His name. I was in the post office and putting some stamps on my tax returns (having a wonderful day, no doubt) when I heard a man using the name of the Lord in vain. I turned around to see who he was talking to and was surprised to see that he was cursing the stamp machine. He was damning that machine in God's name because it wouldn't give him the stamps that he wanted. I thought to myself, "he doesn't know God". I wanted to tell him that the stamp machine is just a machine, and God had nothing to do with jamming it.

The Bible says that God doesn't overlook someone who curses His name. It's one of the Ten Commandments. Exodus 20:7 says, "You shall not take the name of the Lord your God in vain, for the Lord will not hold him guiltless who takes His name in vain."

Do you want to get God's attention? Curse His name, and you've got it, although it's not the kind of attention that you'd really want. Try getting God's attention by praising His name. The Bible says that He inhabits the praises of His people. Become a worshipper of God. He will respond to you. There is power in His name – His name is a strong tower. The righteous run into it and they are safe.

3. Our Conversation. Not only does God record our character and our contemplation, but verse 16 also mentions conversation. "Then those who feared the Lord spoke to one another." The Lord listened to what they were saying and He was pleased.

4. Our Company. God takes note of our company. "They spoke to one another." We are not to give up meeting together (Hebrews 10:25). We're part of the body of Christ, and we need to get together. And when we get together, it's not to talk about the latest hot investment. We are to speak about the goodness of God. What is God doing in our lives? What's God doing in my family? What's God doing in my business? In my community? In my church?

Most of us wouldn't even know each other if it hadn't been for Jesus. I wouldn't know many of my friends if it hadn't been for Jesus Christ saving their lives and redeeming them, and they wouldn't know me for the same reason. I wouldn't know or be married to my wife, Joy—the list could go and on. God records the company that we keep.

When I was in grade school, my teacher drew a detention square in the corner of the blackboard. If your name was written inside that detention square, you had the privilege of staying after school for 15 minutes. If there was check beside your name, it meant another 15 minutes. A second check would warrant an additional quarter hour. A third check meant – you guessed it – 15 more minutes. If there was a fourth check, your parents came and you were dismissed from school. I remember it like it was yesterday. Why do I remember so clearly? Because sometimes my name was up there.

What does God write in His book of remembrance? I'll

tell you what He doesn't write down. He doesn't record your sins – they are under the blood. God is recording your character, your contemplations, your conversations, and the company you keep. He wants to reward you for how you honor His name. He is recording the things that other people haven't noticed: the little deeds that you do, the acts of kindness that you show. God has them written down.

Jesus said if you give a cup of cold water in His name, you will be rewarded for it. If you are serving God's people, or providing for your family, or struggling to maintain your testimony on the job - God is keeping track of you. God remembers those who are His own, and you have the assurance that God will reward you in His time.

REWARD #2:
THE AFFIRMATION THAT JESUS REJOICES OVER HIS OWN
"They shall be Mine," says the Lord of hosts, "on the day that I make them My jewels. And I will spare them as a man spares his own son who serves him." (Malachi 3:17)

There is one thing I look forward to as God's servant. I eagerly anticipate the day when Christ will rejoice over me. "They will be Mine," says the Lord, "on the day that I make them My jewels." The NIV uses the phrase, "my treasured possession." It speaks of something very valuable; something that is rare and priceless.

You are valuable to God. If you've been told you are worthless, or you feel rejected by family or friends, then listen to the truth: God calls you His jewel, His treasured possession. It is rewarding to serve the Lord because He values you.

I first met Joy when I was 18. We fell in love, and at the ripe old age of 19, I got up the nerve to ask her to marry me. Like most college students, I didn't have much money. I went to a jeweler to pick out a ring, and explained my financial status.

He said, "No problem. We work with people like you all the time." So, I looked in the display case, and I found a ring. You practically needed a magnifying glass to see the diamond, but it was all I could afford. I won't tell you how much it cost because it's embarrassing now, but in those days in was a lot of money for a poor college student. I made payments every month on that ring until I finally had it paid off.

Joy has worn that ring for 28 years now. It's a possession that she treasures. We thought about maybe making some changes to the ring, and she said, "No, I'm going to keep that ring because that's the ring you gave me over 28 years ago when you asked me to marry you."

God sees us that way. We are valuable to Him. We may have flaws, and we may not be all that spectacular to anybody else, but we are His treasured possession. That's a reward.

REWARD #3: THE ANTICIPATION THAT JESUS WILL RETURN FOR HIS OWN

Then you shall again discern between the righteous and the wicked, between one who serves God and one who does not serve Him. (Malachi 3:18)

The third reward in this passage is the anticipation that Jesus will return for His own. Jesus is going to come soon. And if you wonder if it's worth serving the Lord, you will find out when He comes. Verse 18 states that on that day, we will see the distinction between the wicked and the righteous, between one who serves God and one who doesn't.

When is this going to happen? Here is a prophecy from Malachi, in the Old Testament, about the second coming of Christ. The prophet is saying that Jesus will come again and you will know when He comes. There will be a reward.

1 Thessalonians 4:13-18 is a passage that deals with the subject in more detail. But I will tell you this—Jesus, who fed the five thousand, walked on water, and did all of those things, died

on the cross for you, rose again from the grave, ascended into heaven, and is going to come again. The trumpet is going to sound, and the dead in Christ will rise first, and we who are alive will be caught up in the air to meet Him. The Bible says to encourage one another with this. Does it pay to serve the Lord? Absolutely, absolutely, absolutely!

I read once that Albert Einstein was traveling on a train, and the ticket-taker came through to punch the passenger's tickets. When he came to Einstein, the scientist couldn't find his ticket. He searched in his wallet and his coat pockets and inside his briefcase. Then Einstein got down on all fours and looked on the floor. The ticket was lost.

"Sir, I know who you are," the ticket-taker said. "You're Albert Einstein, and I know that you wouldn't have just gotten on board this train without paying. Don't worry about it." He then continued down the aisle, punching tickets. Passing by again, he saw Einstein down on the floor of the train, still searching for his ticket.

"Mr. Einstein, it's okay," the ticket-taker assured him. "I know who you are. I believe you have a ticket for this train."

Albert Einstein stood up and said, "I know who I am, too. I'm Albert Einstein. But I've got to find this ticket because I have no idea where I'm going!"

Because of Jesus, I know who I am. Because of Jesus, I know where I'm going. How about you? We belong to Him – He knows us by name. We are valuable to Him – His priceless jewels. And He is returning soon to take us home. The rewards of serving Him are worth it.

Further Study and Reflection
ADDITIONAL SCRIPTURES:

Psalm 37:1-5   Proverbs 1:7   John 10:27
II Corinthians 5:17   1 Thessalonians 4:13

QUESTIONS TO PONDER:
1. Was there a special recognition you received growing up? How did it make you feel?

2. According to this chapter, what are some of the rewards of serving Jesus?

3. If you were to give a testimony about God's faithfulness in your life, what one thing could you praise the Lord for?

4. What is the something that you are asking and believing God for today?

CHAPTER EIGHT

LIVING TODAY IN LIGHT OF TOMORROW

MALACHI 4:1-6

"For you who fear my name, the Sun of Righteousness will rise with healing in his wings."
Malachi 4:2 NLT

The following is a true story about two good friends, Art and Walt. Both were successful entrepreneurs, with lots of creative ideas and growing capital. Both were starting to make a name for themselves. One day, Walt called his buddy and announced, "Hey, I've got a great idea, and I'm going to come and pick you up.'"

Walt pulled into Art's driveway in a brand new convertible. Filled with curiosity, Art climbed into the car. Walt drove and drove. After 45 minutes, he pulled into an orange grove and turned off the engine. There the two friends sat, surrounded by orange trees.

Incredulous, Art asked Walt, "What in the world are we doing out here?"

"Get out of the car," Walt replied. I want you to see this!"

"Can you see it?" Walt asked as the two surveyed the orchard.

"See what?" Art retorted. "All I see are some orange trees."

"No, no, no!" Walt said, shaking his head. "I don't see orange trees. I see a family fun park!"

Convinced that his friend had lost his mind, Art replied, "I don't see any family fun park."

Walt was adamant. "Art, I want you in with me on the ground floor of this thing. We're going to build a family fun park here. People will bring their families and have picnics and enjoy rides and have a great time!"

"Who in the world would drive 45 miles out into the country for a family fun park?" Art asked.

"Hey listen," Walt said, ignoring his friend's lack of enthusiasm. "I need you to get involved in this. I want you to invest some of your money."

Art didn't even have to think that proposal over. "Absolutely not. It's the stupidest idea I've ever heard in my life. Take me home."

Walt tried in vain to revisit the subject a couple of times. But Art's response each time was a resounding "NO!"

Brushing his friend's wild idea aside, Art turned his attention back to Art Linkletter's House Party, his successful radio show. And Walt Disney went ahead and bought that orange orchard and made Disneyland out of it. Maybe you've heard of the place.

Art Linkletter later admitted, "If only I'd seen what Walt had seen, I'd have put my money into that investment and I would be a wealthy man today." Hindsight, as they say, is 20-20.

As a student, wouldn't you like to know what was going to be on the final exam before you took it? Then you could say, "If I only knew the right questions, then I'd know what to study. Do I have to read this book? If I only knew the ten questions that he was going to ask from the book, then I wouldn't have to read the book."

I'm sure that farmers wished they knew how the crop was going to turn out. If they knew it would be a bumper year, they would invest in new equipment. If they knew the harvest would be lean, then they would cut back.

Imagine what it would be like if investors knew which stocks were going to shoot through the ceiling, and which ones would drop like a rock in the next six months. What a financial bonanza it would be if we could only predict the future.

Can we live today in light of tomorrow? God knows the future—nothing catches Him by surprise. He doesn't say, "Oh, I didn't see that coming!" Not only does God know the future, but He holds the future in His hands. He is in control of tomorrow. And He gives us insight into what's going to take place down line. We do not have to live like those who don't have a clue because the Bible is full of information and insight.

Malachi 4 is the last chapter in the last book of the Old

Testament. The prophet Malachi came with a message to prepare God's people for the first coming of Christ. For twenty-first century Christians, his message is to prepare our hearts for the second coming of Christ.

There is a 400 year gap between the Old and New Testaments. The words of Malachi are the last that God speaks for four centuries. After these six verses in Malachi 4, God remains silent until the coming of John the Baptist. As the days of the old covenant come to an end, God speaks to all generations about living in the light of the future.

> "For behold, the day is coming, burning like an oven, and all the proud, yes, all who do wickedly will be stubble. And the day which is coming shall burn them up," says the Lord of hosts, "that will leave them neither root nor branch. But to you who fear My name the Sun of Righteousness shall arise with healing in His wings; and you shall go out and grow fat like stall-fed calves. You shall trample the wicked, for they shall be ashes under the soles of your feet on the day that I do this," says the Lord of hosts. "Remember the Law of Moses, My servant, which I commanded him in Horeb for all Israel, with the statutes and judgments. Behold, I will send you Elijah the prophet before the great and dreadful day of the Lord. And He will turn the hearts of the fathers to the children, and the hearts of the children to their fathers, lest I come and strike the earth with a curse." (Malachi 4:1-6)

God has some amazing things to say in this passage to those who have ears to hear and eyes to see. He desires to give us insight about tomorrow that will help us live today.

Pay close attention to verse 2: "But to you who fear My name, the Sun of Righteousness shall arise with healing in His wings." Malachi, the last of the Old Testament prophets, is prophesying the second coming of Christ in this passage—before His first coming has come to pass! This is hard for us to comprehend, but God doesn't view time like we do. God sees beyond the here and now.

Read carefully through Chapter four. What phrase do you find repeated again and again? The day, that day, the day, that day – it is mentioned several times and is the focus of the passage. Malachi is describing the day when Jesus Christ will return for His Bride.

There are three prophetic announcements that I see revealed in Chapter Four.

BE AWARE...OF THE FINAL DAY OF RETRIBUTION

First of all, Malachi tells us to be aware of the final day of retribution. The word "retribution" means "judgment." There will be a final judgment. This truth is serious. And it's sobering. The judgment is going to be severe for those who don't know the Lord. Verse 1 states that, for those who resist, "the day which is coming shall burn them up." This final day of retribution will burn like a fiery furnace.

I believe that God has given us prophets for today—men who boldly call us to get our lives in order for the return of Christ. When I was a young man, I met David Wilkerson at a youth rally. And he put the fear of God in me! He is the man who started Teen Challenge, a national organization that helps people escape the snare of drug and alcohol abuse. Teen Challenge works because God is the center of the equation. People are delivered from their addictions because their focus is on getting their lives right with God.

David Wilkerson also wrote the book entitled, "The Cross and the Switchblade." The book describes David's ministry to the gangs of New York City. The story begins with David serving at a small church in Pennsylvania. David decided to quit watching television and began to pray for an hour every evening.

One night during his prayer time, David looked up and his eyes fell upon the cover of a national magazine. His attention was riveted by a photo of gang members in New York City. Even though David had never been to New York, God gave him a burden for those gang members. Urged on by the hand of God, he got in his car and drove to the city. David didn't know where to stay, so he slept in his car.

His ministry there was not easy. His life was threatened. He was not accepted by the kids he'd come to help. But David Wilkerson kept on, and as a result, many of the gang members came to know the Lord. Drug addicts and heroine addicts and prostitutes gave their lives to Jesus because of this man.

David Wilkerson still ministers in New York City. He pastors a church in Times Square, in the heart of the city where pornography, drugs, and prostitution abound. God has called this man to be a prophetic voice that speaks to the conscience of the church in America. And David Wilkerson has not held back. He is faithful to point out our nation's sins and to call both the lost and the redeemed back to the Truth.

One example Wilkerson points to is the deterioration of our schools since prayer was removed from the classroom. Forty years ago, the top offenses in public school were: talking in class, running in the halls, chewing gum, and littering. Today, rape, robbery, arson, and even murder are the offenses dealt with in our schools. What a big difference the absence of a "little" thing like prayer has made!

We live in a dark day, a day that Malachi prophesied about. Today, the Ten Commandments have been replaced with metal detectors and campus police. Our children can obtain birth control or even get an abortion without any parental consent or notification. In some places, neither students nor their teachers feel safe at school. I'm not just talking about shootings in the inner city—the violence has spread to the suburbs and rural areas. But a greater darkness than this is sweeping our land; the evil of child abuse and child pornography. Because of the internet, we have easy access to pornography in our very homes.

Even believers can be pulled into these unspeakable practices. I know, because I have to deal with people who struggle with these terrible issues. We live in a day where children are violated, right here in America. But there is going to be a day of retribution, a day of judgment. The consequences of sin will finally be reaped.

Sometimes, the consequences for sin are immediate. For example, sexually transmitted diseases are a consequence of sin. Drunk-driving accidents are a consequence of sin. But it doesn't always work that way. We all know people who are living in sin, and they seem to be getting along fine. In fact, they're having a great time doing wrong. These people may not face the consequences of their sins in the present, but eventually there will be an accounting, a day of retribution. It is the "great and dreadful day of the Lord" spoken of in this passage.

Romans 1 talks about the present penalties of violating God's will. But Malachi 4 points to a fiery, final day that is going to come. 2 Thessalonians 1:6-8 is another passage that describes how God deals with those who fail to respond to the Gospel.

We live in dark times. As we contemplate the future, it's important to understand that there is a final judgment to come. We do ourselves no favors by skipping over this part of the Bible and pretending it isn't there.

BE ASSURED...OF THE FUTURE DAY OF RESTORATION

Not only will there be a day of retribution, but there will be a day of restoration. Look at verse 2, "But to you who fear My name the Sun of Righteousness shall arise with healing in His wings."

Do you respect and reverence the name of the Lord? Do you worship God? Do you love Him? Good if you do! For God will not only punish the wicked, He will also reward the righteous. There will be a day of restoration for those who fear His name. And when Christ returns, He will bring healing – the final healing – of this culture.

We've contaminated our rivers and polluted the air we breathe. But there is going to be a day when everything is going to be restored, and made perfect and beautiful, as it was in the beginning. The land itself will be healed.

In John 8:12, Jesus said, "I am the light of the world. He who follows Me shall not walk in darkness, but have the light of life." Jesus is the Son who gives spiritual light to those who follow Him. Malachi refers to the Sun of Righteousness. The Sun shines in the sky and brings physical light to us. The two concepts are related. There is going to be a day when the Son comes and the Sun of Righteousness will have healing in His wings.

This healing is available to us today. The fruit of salvation is wholeness. Jesus came to make us whole – in body, soul, and spirit. And we do experience His healing, even though we must continue to live in a broken-down, toxic world. We won't receive the ultimate healing until that day of restoration comes. And it is coming!

Do you suffer with the difficulties of sickness or pain? Have you felt the grief of losing a loved one? Then cling to the promise that a day is coming when there will be no more tears, or sickness, or sorrow. On that day, the Sun of Righteousness will come with healing in His wings.

Jesus will turn our darkness into light. He will turn our sickness into health. He will turn our sorrow into joy. Such is the day of restoration.

I heard about a little boy who sat up all night wondering where the sun went. Finally, it dawned on him. And the sun will come up. And so it will be for us—the S-O-N will come up! All the darkness, and all the sin, will flee away.

Note 1 John 3:2. "We know that when He is revealed, we shall be like Him, for we shall see Him as He is." Some of you are going through tough times. Life has not been easy. You feel like you're going uphill all the time, peddling as fast as you can and you feel like you're going nowhere. But one of these days, He will break through the clouds, and He will come. The Sun of Righteousness will come.

This is what the Bible teaches, and this is what we believe. Maybe it's news to you, or perhaps you've heard it a thousand times – but it is the truth. The Sun of Righteousness will come and everything that stands against Him – the devil and his angels, the demons that harass you day after day – will vanish. Forever.

BE ANTICIPATING...THE FANTASTIC RAPTURE

Malachi calls us to anticipate a fantastic rapture. He describes this event in a number of ways, but notice verse 5: "Behold I will send you Elijah the prophet before the coming of the great and dreadful day of the Lord."

Now, some think that Elijah was John the Baptist, who prepared the way for the first coming of Jesus Christ. Other scholars go to the book of Revelation and point out that there are two witnesses during the tribulation period in the streets of Jerusalem, and they identify one witness as Elijah.

Whichever the case may be, the point is that Jesus Christ, the Sun of Righteousness (or the bright and morning star, as the New Testament refers to Him) is coming, and we need to be ready for Him.

Joy and I went on vacation recently. One restful day, we decided to have a late lunch at a hotel. When we entered the massive dining room, the place was empty. We were sitting there, all alone. After we placed our order, another couple came in and were seated—right next to us.

Now, I'm a friendly guy and it didn't take me long to turn around and introduce myself. "Good to see you," I chatted away. "How long have you been here? Blah, blah, blah." The woman was friendly enough, but the man really got into conversation.

I discovered that he had just retired from the aerospace industry. I tried to think about everything I knew concerning rockets and jets and asked him questions along those lines (which took about 30 seconds). We then talked about our families and where we lived, and finally he asked me the big question – "And what do you do for a living?"

So I told him. His transformation was immediate and miraculous. My new friend suddenly got religion and said: "Oh, my wife and I go to church occasionally as well."

This is interesting, I thought. We kept chatting until we'd finished our meals. As we walked out of the restaurant, the man turned to me and asked, "Do you believe in the rapture? What does it mean, anyway?"

Before I could speak, he continued, "I'm reading this series called, 'Left Behind' by Tim LaHaye. It's all new to me, I've never been taught any of this. Is it true? Is it really going to happen like that?"

"Well, you understand that the 'Left Behind' series is a fictional story,' I explained, "but it's based on Biblical truths. It's the author's view of what could happen and how it might come about. But, the point is, it will happen."

Are you ready for the rapture? Admittedly, the word "rapture" is not in Scripture, but the concept is one of being "caught up in the clouds with Him," and it is a Biblical teaching.

1 Thessalonians 4:15-18 is the foundational text for the rapture. Verse 17 says, "Then we who are alive and remain shall be caught up together with them in the clouds to meet the Lord in the air. And thus we shall always be with the Lord."

Let me illustrate with some possible scenarios. Mark and Jim are working together on a project. They've worked at the same office for 10 years. Everybody knows that Mark is a believer in Jesus Christ. He has attempted to speak to Jim on several occasions, but Jim doesn't want to hear. Jim turns around and Mark's not there. He was there just a moment ago, but he's gone. The rapture.

Michelle and Jennifer have been friends since kindergarten. Their lockers are right next to each other. They live in the same neighborhood, and have been on the same soccer team as kids. Michelle has talked to Jennifer a number of times about coming to church with her. She's invited her to youth group, but Jennifer has made excuses every time. One day, they're talking to each other in between classes at school. Jennifer opens her locker and when she turns around to say something else to Michelle, she's not there. The rapture.

Dan is playing golf with Walt. They hit the links every Monday afternoon, and they love it. They joke and tease, and while they don't really bet, occasionally they'll challenge each other with whoever gets the best score has to pay for lunch. Walt has talked to Dan innumerable times about Jesus Christ, and has tried to be a consistent witness with his life. Walt steps up to the tee. Dan is watching him. Walt drives the ball down the fairway, and Dan keeps his eye on ball to spot where it lands. When he turns to look back toward the tee box, Walt is gone. The rapture.

Those are just some of the possible scenarios of what's going to take place.

I recently officiated at a memorial service for Francis Moody, one of the members of our church. For the believer, a funeral is like a graduation service – is marks a time of transition and is a time of rejoicing. During the funeral, I talked about Christ and His return and the promise of heaven. With family and friends gathered together, we ushered Francis into glory.

After the funeral, I went and spoke to a group of couples who are engaged. As I was helping these couples prepare for a lifetime of wedded bliss, I got a phone call informing me that another dear friend had just died and gone to be with the Lord.

We take life for granted, and assume that we always have tomorrow. When I got up that morning, I had no idea what would happen. I had my schedule mapped out, but I didn't know that the day would end like that. It reminded me to live in anticipation of a fantastic rapture. One day, God is going to intervene and return for His own. We don't fear this. If we are in right relationship to the Lord, it is something that we can eagerly anticipate.

THE PRACTICAL APPLICATIONS

So how do we live today in light of tomorrow? Three practical applications.

Be Certain About Your Commitment

Have you given your life to Christ? It's the only way to insure peace of mind as you face the prospect of tomorrow. Malachi 4 speaks of "the great and dreadful day of the Lord." It is both great and terrible. It will prove great if you are a believer, and something to dread if you are not. Face the future with confidence by committing your life to Jesus Christ and remaining committed to Him.

Be Careful About Your choices

At the end of his life and ministry, Joshua stood before the children of Israel. He wanted to address the next generation and equip them for the future. This man of faith challenged the nation by saying, "Choose this day who you will serve" (Joshua 24:15).

That is the question I want to ask you. "Whom are you going to serve?" Elijah confronted the prophets of Baal in a classic showdown in 1 Kings 18. The lone prophet stood before God's people, who had been worshipping idols and said, "Listen, which God are you going to follow? Are you going to follow the God of heaven, or are you going to follow these idols?" The choice is yours.

The apostle Paul stood in front of royalty, and after taking advantage of the opportunity to present the Gospel, he told them point blank, "You need to choose." The book of Acts says that King Agrippa was "almost persuaded" (Acts 27:28). Almost but not quite. Be careful about your choices.

Be Clear About your Convictions

Do you have godly convictions or beliefs? Are your convictions displayed through godly behavior?

We must be certain about our commitment, careful about our choices, and clear about our convictions. As a follower of Jesus Christ, I don't have to live under a curse. I choose to live under the blessing of God. Malachi lays out for us how we can be blessed in our lives, how we can turn night into day, how we can turn sorrow into joy, how we can turn the struggles of life into victories.

CONCLUSION

Ask Russell Chandler about living today in light of tomorrow. He'll never forget the morning when he woke up at 4:30 and found himself on the bedroom floor. His wife hadn't pushed him out of bed, but there he was sprawled across the floor.

An earthquake that registered 6.6 on the Richter scale had been the culprit. Russell lived in the Northridge area of Los Angeles, and his neighborhood had been right at the epicenter of this particular quake. Russell only suffered a tumble out of bed, but many of his neighbors weren't so fortunate. Fifty lives were claimed during that sudden disaster.

How did Russell respond to the experience? "It was a wake-up call for me to check out my life and get things in order," he said. "I realized that I was living for myself and not even concerned about tomorrow. Even though the media had warned us with plenty of hype to be prepared, I didn't prepare one thing. I'm more prepared today."

How much more should you and I prepare for the tomorrow that God has for us? Let us begin walking today in the light He has given us for tomorrow.

Further Study and Reflection:
ADDITIONAL SCRIPTURES:

Matthew 26:64 Acts 1:11   Matthew 24:36
1 Thessalonians 5:2   James 5:8
I Timothy 6:14   I John 2:28

QUESTIONS TO PONDER:
1. What is one of the most memorable trips you have ever taken??

2. What are the three prophetic announcements in Malachi Chapter 4?

3. In your opinion, what recent events point to Christ's return?

4. What impact should the return of Jesus Christ have on a person's life?